Becoming
A Contagious Christian

Becoming A Contagious Christian

Bill Hybels

Alpha
Aylesbury, Bucks HP22 5BL
England

Becoming A Contagious Christian

Special edition

Published jointly by Zondervan Publishing House
Grand Rapids, Michigan 49530 and Scripture Press,
Raans Road, Amersham-on-the-Hill, Bucks HP6 6JQ.

Requests for information should be addressed to:
Zondervan Publishing House, Grand Rapids, Michigan 49530.

ISBN 1 898938 29 6

In the interests of privacy, some names have been changed.

Designed and Produced in England for
ALPHA an imprint of
SP Trust, Wendover Road, Stoke Mandeville,
Aylesbury, Bucks HP22 5BL by
Nuprint Ltd, Station Road, Harpenden, Herts AL5 4SE.

To Tom Giesler:
Whose transformed life
serves notice to the world
that God is alive and well.

To Effa Mittelberg:
Whose contagious Christianity
has influenced her entire family
for four generations—and counting.

Contents

Acknowledgements

Thanks for pausing here as we acknowledge the support and help we've received from some highly contagious Christians. Topping the list are our wives, Lynne Hybels and Heidi Mittelberg, who've been our consistent partners in ministry and great encouragers as we've written this book.

Next, deep appreciation goes to our friend and coworker, Lee Strobel, who generously gave of his time and expertise to sharpen our thoughts, as well as to John Sloan and John Raymond at Zondervan for their valuable editorial input.

We'd also like to thank our administrative assistants, Jean Blount and Laura Daughtry, for their faithful support.

Finally, we owe a debt of gratitude to the following people for their encouragement and constructive criticism of various parts of the manuscript: Julie Harney, Chad Meister, Brad Mitchell, Bob and Gretchen Passantino, Garry Poole, and Russ Robinson.

SECTION ONE

Why Become a Contagious Christian?

CHAPTER ONE

People Matter To God

Not long after Tom stepped onto the sailboat, it became clear that he was a first-class sailor, a fierce competitor, and someone who thrived on living at the edge of adventure.

Beyond that, this latest member of our racing crew had an infectious personality. He wanted the music turned up loud, lots of friends around, and plenty of excitement after the race. He wanted to win, but he wanted to have a good time doing it.

I hardly knew Tom when I asked him to join us. As our friendship developed, I found out that he was an all-or-nothing kind of individual. When he believed in something and was excited about it, there was no stopping him. But if he wasn't interested, there was almost no way to get him started.

And therein was the challenge. You see, Tom had little time for spiritual matters of any kind.

Then one night Tom showed up for our regatta with his arm in a sling. When I asked him what had happened, he explained that he had been out racing go-carts the night before, had imbibed too much alcohol, had got a bit out of control, and ended up getting into a fight.

By this time he knew I was a minister, so he half-kiddingly asked if I could help him out by praying over him.

"Maybe sometime," I replied, "but right now I have a Scripture verse for you."

"All right," he said, "what is it?"

I said, "The Bible says in Galatians 6:7 that 'a man reaps what he sows.' "

To my surprise, Tom seemed stunned. "It doesn't really say that, does it?" he asked.

"It absolutely does," I told him. "It says that if you want to sow the kind of seed you were sowing last night, you're going to reap the kind of sling you're wearing today."

"You're putting me on!" he shot back.

"I'm not kidding you," I assured him, "and I think maybe you ought to commit that verse to memory!"

Over the next few days, I'd chide him a little by asking if he'd learned it yet. Before long, he'd just look me in the eye and quote it.

In fact, that whole incident became somewhat of a standing joke between us that summer, and it opened up the door to some conversations about spiritual matters. The following season Tom showed a few more signs that he was willing to take it a bit further.

One night when we were having dinner in a restaurant he asked me, "How does a person go about getting a Bible? I've thought about trying to read one, but I didn't know if regular stores sell them."

"Well, I could probably fix you up with one," I told him, trying to be nonchalant about the fact that finally, after two years of prayer and relationship-building, he was starting to display some genuine interest.

Later that fall, Tom actually drove a couple of hundred miles from Michigan to Chicago in order to visit our church and to spend some time hanging out at my house and talking together.

After he got back home, he called me and said, "I feel different on the inside. It seems like I'm starting to fit some *puzzle pieces together. I don't know how it's all going to turn out, but I really like what's happening to me, even if I don't completely understand it."*

One evening after a two-hour talk about what it means to be a Christian, I told him, "Tommy, you're going to make a great Christian someday. You're honest to the core, flat-out dedicated to whatever you commit yourself to, and more concerned about what's true than about what other people think."

He conceded that I might be right. But he wasn't ready. He was in the process and moving in the right direction, but he wasn't about to sign on any dotted lines. Not yet.

I'll never forget those talks with Tom. They were unpredictable, they were risky, they were exhilarating, they were give-and-take, they were up-and-down. And they reminded me of something I'd known for a long time: There's nothing in life that's as exciting as befriending, loving, and leading wayward people toward faith in Christ. Nothing.

In their heart of hearts, I think all true followers of Christ long to become contagious Christians. Though unsure about how to do so or the risks involved, deep down they sense that there isn't anything as rewarding as opening a person up to God's love and truth.

But though we might like the idea of having a spiritual impact on others, we won't take decisive action unless we first raise our motivation level. And one of the best ways to do that is to get God's perspective on the matter.

Let's begin with two lessons, both from unexpected sources. One is from the realm of science, the other is from the world of business. The first describes the way things are. The second prescribes the way things ought to be.

A surprising source

First, there is the Anthropic Principle. It's creating a lot of controversy these days among intellectuals. "Of course," you say, "the Anthropic Principle. I was just reading about that last night before I went to bed!"

In their heart of hearts, I think all true followers of Christ long to become contagious Christians. Though unsure about how to do so or the risks involved, deep down they sense that there isn't anything as rewarding as opening a person up to God's love and truth.

Simply stated, the Anthropic Principle implies that when we look at the world around us, it would *seem*, at least at first blush, that the universe was somehow *designed* to support and nourish human life.

This concept, which is very prevalent in the world of secular science and philosophy, didn't originate with Christian scholars. But the evidence points so overwhelmingly toward this apparent design in the universe that it's virtually undeniable by experts of every religious and nonreligious stripe. This has sent sceptics scurrying to find some sort of natural explanation for this apparently supernatural phenomenon.

Here are a few of the hard facts:

- Raise or lower the universe's rate of expansion by even one part in a million, and it would have ruled out the possibility of life.
- If the average distance between stars were any greater, planets like earth would not have been

formed; any smaller, the planetary orbits necessary for life would not have occurred.

- If the ratio of carbon to oxygen had been slightly different than it is, none of us would have been here to breathe the air.
- Change the tilt of the earth's axis slightly in one direction, and we would freeze. Change it the other direction, and we'd burn up.
- Suppose the earth had been a bit closer or further from the sun, or just a little larger or smaller, or if it rotated at a speed any different from the one we're spinning at right now. Given any of these changes, the resulting temperature variations would be completely fatal.

So the lesson we can draw from the Anthropic Principle is this: *Someone* must have gone to a lot of effort to make things just right so that you and I could be here to

---

Being the ever-obedient spiritual heavyweight that I am, I did what any serious-minded, devoted follower of Christ would do. I called one of those internal time-outs and said to the Lord, "Hold on a minute! Let's not get carried away!"

---

enjoy life. In short, modern science points to the fact that *we must really matter to God!*

A lesson from business

Now let's move from science to the world of business. Did you know there's been a radical transformation in this arena during the last few years that provides an important lesson for Christians?

Cutting-edge management experts have been talking about these developments in grandiose terms. For example, in *Thriving On Chaos*, Tom Peters refers to this transformation as a "customer revolution". Ken Blanchard, author of the enormously successful book, *The One-Minute Manager*, has been crisscrossing the United States talking about what he calls "the upside-down pyramid". What is this change that they feel is so critical for all of corporate America to hear?

Are you ready for this? Hold onto your wingtips: Businesses, if they're going to be successful for the long haul, must pull their attention off of themselves and refocus their energies on their only reason for existence—to serve their customers.

Now, before we chide them for going to great lengths to state the obvious, let's note that this advice is sorely needed. How many times do you feel frustrated when you're trying to get basic service at a garage, restaurant, bank, bakery, or department store? The natural tendency for these organisations, both big and small, is to become ingrown. Employees begin burning up their energy on internal problems, petty policy disputes, and staff-related strife. And all too often this happens while the customer stands at the checkout counter patiently waiting to be served.

So along come experts like Peters and Blanchard with a challenge that is simple and profound. It's time to turn over the corporate pyramid, they say, and get back to serving the person "at the top"—and that's the customer, *not* the boss. We must work to develop a "customer obsession".

It's not hard to see that both the problems and the solutions of the business world have close cousins within the Christian community. We can get so easily entangled and ensnared in the internal issues, questions, and personal situations in our churches that it's hard to remember that the primary reason we remain on this planet is to reach the people "out there". Just like commercial organisations need to get their focus off themselves, we as individual Christians and collective churches need to recalibrate our sights on the target God has given us: spiritually lost people.

So if the lesson from science is that people matter to God, then the lesson from business is *they'd better matter to us, too*. Only as we begin to value those outside our Christian circles will we be truly fulfilled and functioning according to God's purpose for us.

But let's be honest. It's hard to keep our focus. Our tendency is to drift away from genuinely valuing the spiritually confused. We're quick to forget how much they matter to God.

An eye-opening interchange

I was reminded of this recently on a trip when I bumped into an old acquaintance. He was a man I knew to be a churchgoer, so to get a conversation going, I said to him, "Well, are you looking forward to Easter Sunday?"

As casually as I had asked the question, he replied, "No, I'm not. As a matter of fact, I never go to church at Easter."

"You're kidding!" I said. "You don't go to church on Easter Sunday? You can get arrested for that!"

Ignoring my attempt at humour, he said with some intensity, "I don't go to church at Easter because I can't stand to see all those 'oncers'. You know, the 'annuals', all the people who only come around once a year. They get themselves all dressed up to make their appearance, and they mess everything up at my church, especially the car park. Who do these people think they're fooling?

They're not fooling me and they're certainly not fooling God! This has bothered me so much over the years that I just quit going to church on Easter Sunday. I have no use for 'oncers'."

Although he didn't say it directly, I thought to myself, "Not only does *he* have no use for these people, I'll bet he's convinced that *God* doesn't have any use for them, either."

And you know, as much as I hate to admit it, it's not uncommon for people like me—and maybe like you—to fall prey to similar value judgments. We all tend to make armchair assessments of who God has use for and who He doesn't. And before we know it, we've reduced our mental list of those God really cares about to our own little group of select people who happen to look just

---

Jesus' stories in Luke 15 tell us that you have never locked eyes with another human being who isn't valuable to God.

---

like us. That list almost never includes the people "out there" who aren't part of the church.

Can you see how dangerous this is? Once we've bought into this line of reasoning, we've imperceptibly but effectively removed any hope of getting motivated to spread God's message of grace. After all, if these people don't matter that much to God, why should we get all worked up about trying to reach them?

An age-old issue

This kind of thinking is not new among God's people. We see the same attitudes surfacing in various places throughout the Bible. In fact, one of the central thrusts of Jesus' ministry was to address this issue and challenge His would-be followers to change their view of those outside the family of God.

One day while Jesus was teaching in a sizeable metropolitan area, He found Himself surrounded by a large crowd of irreligious people. Oncers. Undesirables. The unconvinced. The spiritually confused. The morally bankrupt people of the town. People God wouldn't possibly have any use for!

Off to the side was a huddle of religious leaders who were shaking their heads and talking to each other in muffled tones. They were complaining about the fact that Jesus, who claimed to be the Son of the holy God, was hanging out with—well, let's just say it—*those* kinds of people.

Jesus knew exactly what they were thinking. So He moved the whole procession over to where those in the "holy huddle" were standing. Then, in a steady but forceful tone, he began to tell a pointed and powerful series of stories.

Lost and found

"There was once a man who owned a hundred sheep," He said. "And while he was tending his sheep, one of those sheep wandered away. So the shepherd left the ninety-nine behind and went out and searched for the one that was lost. And he kept on searching until he finally found it. He tenderly picked up the sheep, put it around his shoulders, and carried it back to the flock. Then he called some of his shepherd friends and said, 'Let's have a party. I found my wandering sheep!' "

Jesus paused for a moment. Everyone was still listening. "Then there was a woman who had ten coins," He continued. "She lost one of them. So she lit a lamp, swept the house, turned over all the furniture, and searched relentlessly until she found it. And when she did, this woman was so happy that she called her friends and asked them to celebrate with her."

Jesus stopped again and looked around. Maybe He wondered if they were still with Him. Then He went on, "There was a man who had two boys, and the younger one got a little cocky. He was longing for adventure and wanted to taste life to the full.

"So he talked his father into giving him his inheritance early, and he headed out into a distant land with his pockets full of money. He found the fast lane and the fast crowd and he did some fast living. But he soon found out that the kind of friends he'd made don't stay around long when the money runs out.

"One day while he was feeding pigs to try to support himself, this disoriented, bankrupt boy finally came to his senses. He decided to go home. He figured he would apologise to his father for his naiveté and immaturity, and then he'd offer to become one of his father's hired hands, since he knew he had forfeited his right to be regarded as his son.

"So he started off for home. His father, who had spent hours each day watching and longing for his son's return, saw him when he was still a long way from the gate. Immediately, the hope-filled father ran down the road to embrace his son. The boy started to say, 'I made an awful mistake, Dad, and I don't deserve to be your son—' But the father interrupted. 'Shhhh, don't talk like that!' he said. 'I'm so glad you're finally home!' He rejoiced and ordered a huge party. He said, 'Invite everyone, kill the fattened calf, and bring out a fresh suit of clothes. My wayward son has come home!' They had a great party!"

Then I think Jesus gazed into the eyes of his listeners

and thought, "There—three stories. That ought to make an impression!"

You see, this is the only recorded time Jesus ever told three parables in a row. Generally, He would perceive some misunderstanding in the minds of people, size it up, and tell a story that would clarify the issue. Then He'd go on until he saw the next area that needed attention.

But not this time. This particular day Jesus was so upset over the discussion the religious leaders were having about who matters to God and who doesn't, that He said, in effect, "I'm going to clear this up once and for all. I never want there to be confusion on this again. I'm going to tell you not one, not two, but three stories—rapid fire—to make sure everybody understands who really matters to God."

Essential elements

There are some common threads that run through these stories in Luke 15. The first is that in each one, *something of great value was missing*, something that really mattered. The missing sheep was very important to the shepherd. It represented a significant part of his livelihood. The lost coin was vital to the woman's survival. Quite possibly she was a widow, and what was at stake was a tenth of her entire estate. And, it goes without saying, the wayward son mattered greatly to his father.

As Jesus' listeners reflected on these stories, I think some of them began to grasp what He was driving at. It must have taken their breath away when the light finally went on in their heads! This is true especially of the religious leaders whose self-righteous attitudes prompted these stories in the first place.

The more sensitive people in the crowd likely started to think, "Wait! Could it be? Here we are looking down our noses because Jesus is hanging out with these fast-lane irreligious types whom we have determined—perhaps prematurely—that God has no use for. And Jesus is showing us through these three simple stories that these people—the wanderers, the lost, the spiritually confused—*actually have value to the heavenly Father!*"

Jesus said He came to earth to "seek and to save the lost." And right before He left He said, "As the Father sent me, now I'm sending you."

When Jesus' listeners put all that together, they were probably crushed by the weight of God's love. A love so large that it could look beyond sins and treasure the wayward people behind them. A love so powerful that it could patiently endure years of resistance, selfish pleasure-seeking, money-chasing, and power-wielding. In the face of all this, God's love says, "Even though you're way off the track, you *still* matter to Me! You really do!"

Conversations on the Cross

The Bible tells us that Jesus was crucified between two thieves. It's important to remember that these two were serious criminals. They didn't crucify people in those days for petty misdimeanours. These thieves had done some heavy-duty damage, and society had decided it had no further use for them.

While they were hanging on crosses, one of them launched into a verbal tirade. He railed against Jesus, saying that if He was really the Son of God, He should come down from the cross and, while He's at it, take them down, too. The other thief, however, opened his eyes to what was really happening. He realised that in just a short time he would face eternity, and he was painfully aware of the kind of life he had lived.

So, finally, he blurted out to the other thief, "Shut up! Can't you see what's going on here? Just keep quiet." Then he turned to Jesus and said, "We're getting exactly what we deserve. But you haven't done anything wrong. Furthermore, you know all about me and my life. So excuse me if this is a silly question, but could somebody like me, who has committed all the sins I've committed, still matter to *anybody*?"

What did Jesus say? Without hesitation, He assured this man, "You matter far more than you can imagine! And because of your faith and your tender, repentant spirit, you'll meet up with me just a little later today in Paradise, where we'll be together for all of eternity!"

It's difficult to comprehend compassion like that, isn't it? Let's face it: It's so unlike your love or mine.

Jesus was so upset over the discussion the religious leaders were having about who matters to God and who doesn't, that He said, in effect, "I never want there to be confusion on this again. I'm going to tell you not one, not two, but three stories—rapid fire—to make sure everybody understands who really matters to God."

A fitness-centre friend

Some time ago, I was studying this passage in Luke 15 and really trying to come to grips with its implications for my life. I was doing my workouts at a fitness centre that had just hired a recent immigrant from India. He was a short, bald man who spoke broken English and was a little unusual. On top of that, he was a devout Muslim. In other words, he wasn't the kind of person I'd have envisioned as a regular golf partner.

But over time I noticed that a lot of the guys at the club didn't want anything to do with this man. Their actions made it clear that he was, to them, a "no count".

There I was, seeing this and trying to grapple with what it means when Jesus says *all* people matter to Him. I knew what it meant *theologically*. That part was easy enough. But what did it mean *practically*?

As you might guess, I had to conclude that if everybody matters to God, then this little Indian Muslim matters to Him, too.

So I started, rather awkwardly at first, to make efforts to befriend him. We talked, we kidded around, we gradually built some rapport. Finally one afternoon I gave him a Bible. And guess what? The next time I saw him he turned around and gave me a Koran!

One day I went to the club after I had been away on a speaking trip. As I was getting dressed to go running, this man came up to me with an anxious look on his face. He said, "Mr Bill, while you were gone something terrible happened. My wife left me, and now I'm all alone. I just don't know what I'm going to do!"

While he was talking, I remembered that he had a small child. It was easy to see the pain he was in, and I think I was the first person he had talked to about this.

As he went on explaining what had happened, I looked into his eyes, and I sensed that the Holy Spirit was leading me to reach out and embrace this man. Being the ever-obedient spiritual heavy-weight that I am, I did what any serious-minded, devoted follower of Christ would do. I called one of those internal time-outs and said to the Lord, "Hold on a minute! Let's not get carried away!"

I told God I had two basic problems with this leading. The first was that I'm not a naturally affectionate person, particularly with men! I'm standing there in the middle of the locker room in my boxer shorts, God's telling me to hug this guy, and I'm thinking, "So how *much* does this man matter, God?"

My second problem had to do with this man's religious orientation. I said, "You are aware, Lord, that this fellow you want me to hug is more than merely a non-worshipper. He is actively worshipping the *competition*!"

As you could have predicted, I didn't get very far in reversing the counsels of the eternal, all-knowing Sovereign of the universe! Instead, I felt as though the Spirit was saying, "I know all about it, Bill. But I want this man to know in the middle of his pain that he matters to the true God. I'm just looking for one of my children to communicate that to him. Will you do it for Me?"

I've got to tell you, it was not an easy step for me. But when I put my arms around the guy, he just broke down and flooded my shoulders with his tears. It was clearly an important moment for him. And, in retrospect, for me, too.

A valuable lesson

Do you see what happened? When I realised how much God cared about this man, it made me care more about him, too. Later on, I admitted to myself how often I, a Christian and a minister, had done the same ugly, unthinkable things the Pharisees had done. I realised that sometimes I carry around little unpublished lists of people who I don't think are very important. You know, the garage attendant who pumps my petrol, the waitress, the hotel staff, the cashier, the person driving the slow-moving car in front of me, the neighbour with the barking dog, the obnoxious intoxicated person sitting next to me on an aeroplane, the person at work who doesn't view the world the way I do. These people don't matter very much, right?

There's nothing like the adventure of being used by God to contagiously spread His love, truth, and life to other people—people who matter deeply to Him.

The truth is, they *do*. They're important to God. Regardless of race, salary, gender, level of education, religious label or lack thereof, they still matter to Him and, therefore, they'd better matter—*really* matter—to me.

When you start to look at others with that kind of attitude, it has a revolutionary effect on the way you treat people. Jesus' stories in Luke 15 tell us that *you have never locked eyes with another human being who isn't valuable to God*. When this fact grips you to the core of your being, you'll never be the same. You will live in awe of the scope and depth and breadth of God's love, and you'll treat people differently.

Worth the effort

"All right," you say, "I'll buy it. People matter to God. But how much?" That question leads us to the second common thread in Jesus' three stories: *that which was missing was important enough to warrant an all-out search*. The sheep got lost, and the shepherd went out looking until he found it. The coin was missing, so the woman hunted through her house until she located it. In the story of the wayward son, the father exercised restraint because he respected his boy's freedom and wanted to let him learn some hard lessons. But his eyes kept scanning the horizon, waiting for the day when his son would come back home. When you really value something, and you lose it, you just naturally want to *search* for it.

And that, I trust, is your central motivation in reading this book. I hope you desire to get involved in what God is doing around the globe to search out and draw in people who are spiritually lost. Jesus said He came to earth to "seek and to save the lost." And right before He left He said, "As the Father sent me, now I'm sending you."

We're on a mission

Deep in every true Christian, there is an awareness that we are on this planet for purposes greater than having a career, paying the bills, loving our families, and fulfilling our role as upstanding citizens. Even going to church and worshipping God—important as these are—sometimes leave us feeling that something is missing. After all, we'll worship God for eternity in heaven; we don't have to be here to do that.

What is it that's absent in the lives of so many believers who are crying out for fulfilment? What on earth is God asking us to do?

God wants us to become contagious Christians—His agents, who will first catch His love and then urgently and infectiously offer it to all who are willing to consider it. This is His primary plan, the one Jesus modelled so powerfully, to spread God's grace and truth person to person until there's an epidemic of changed lives around the world.

And how can you get personally involved in this exciting endeavour? Well, that's the goal of this book: to give you practical steps towards becoming an effective carrier of God's life-changing message.

This effort is clearly beneficial for people who need to be reached, but it seems that all the perks flow *their* way. So a natural question is, "What's in it for *me*?"

That's a legitimate question, and it's the focus of our next chapter, "The Rewards of Contagious Christianity". I think you'll be relieved and excited when you discover the multiple benefits for everyone involved. Spreading our faith to other people is genuinely a win-win proposition.

Perhaps a preview will help illustrate how this is true. In fact, it flows right out of the Luke passage we've been looking at, the final common thread in Jesus' three stories: *Retrievals result in rejoicing*.

Parties in heaven

The shepherd retrieved the sheep and had a party. The woman found the coin and had another party. The son came home and the father had the biggest party of all. And in Luke 15:10 Jesus says, "In the same way, I tell you, there is rejoicing in the presence of the angels of God over *one sinner* who repents."

When I read that text for the first time, I thought of my own life. I was a cocky, rebellious, self-willed seventeen-year-old who thought I knew how to get to heaven by impressing God with my religiosity. But then, through the influence of the Bible and caring Christian friends, it became clear to me that I could never string together enough righteousness to impress a holy God. What I needed was to admit my sins, turn away from them, and trust Christ to be my forgiver, friend, and leader.

I remember exactly where I was standing when I took that critical step. I was at a Christian camp in southern Wisconsin, USA, and I just broke down and repented. According to Luke 15:10, do you know what happened next? All of heaven erupted in a magnificent cosmic celebration. There was an enormous party with the honouree's name on the banner—and it was *mine*! When that dawned on me I remember thinking, "I must *really* matter to God!" It was almost overwhelming to me!

If you're a genuine Christ-follower, the same thing happened when you acknowledged your sin and trusted in Him. Whether last week or forty years ago, all of heaven erupted in a party, and *your* name was on the banner. Do you see how much *you* are treasured by God?

And if you think you know what joy is now, just wait until you're a primary player in the process that leads one of your friends to Christ. You're going to almost *explode* with joy when you take part in that person's celestial celebration. That's only natural, especially when you realise that you actually helped get their name on the banner!

Does that pique your interest? There's nothing like the adventure of being used by God to contagiously spread His love, truth, and life to other people—people who matter deeply to Him. So let's get on with it!

CHAPTER TWO

The Rewards of Contagious Christianity

Have you ever been excited about an idea only to find your enthusiasm fading when you realised the effort it would take to turn the idea into reality?

What about putting away part of your income for retirement or for your child's university education? It's pretty easy to make noble-sounding decisions about appropriate percentages *prior* to actually sitting down with your chequebook. But when you have to make a mortgage payment that takes a third of your income, all of a sudden you're faced with realities that can rob you of your lofty ideals.

Or what about the reconciliation of broken relationships? The best thing to do is to apologise and make amends. After all, that's the path toward renewing friendships. But as good as that sounds, second thoughts often seize us about the time we reach out to pick up the phone or knock on the door.

I could give other examples, but the point is clear: The goal may be noble, the intentions sincere, and the plan in place. But we can still end up not taking action. What holds us back at the point of following through?

Often what's lacking is a clear-headed and open-eyed

examination of the real costs and rewards. Without this, the plan can *sound* good but lack the personal *pull* required to transform ideas into action. You must be convinced that having funds laid aside for later or enjoying a restored relationship is worth the effort and expense.

Weighing the options

Business managers understand this and have developed something called a "cost/benefit analysis" to help them see the whole picture. This is a tool designed to give them a realistic projection of what the proposed course of activity will require on the investment side, as well as what it will yield on the payback side. Armed with that information, they can then make informed decisions and stick to them with minimal surprises along the way.

Each of us does something similar when making a tough choice about which way to turn. Whether it's on paper or just in our minds, we put all the pros on one side of the ledger and the cons on the other. This informal analysis helps us choose the course that makes the most sense.

Jesus suggested a similar approach in Luke 14, where He used two illustrations, one involving constructing a building and the other, going to war. The lesson in both cases was the same: Before embarking on a project, add up what you'll have to invest—"count the cost"—to make sure it's worth the effort and that you'll be able to follow it through to completion.

Now let's relate this to becoming contagious Christians. We've already established that people matter to God and ought to matter to us. We also know that apart from Christ they're lost, and that their inherent worth as humans warrants an all-out search. But has anybody bothered to check lately to see how much these all-out searches cost? The price on the tag doesn't seem to be the bargain it might once have been!

The truth is, it never was. While reaching out to irreligious people may sound good on the surface, you don't have to look very deeply before you realise the actual rescue effort is going to entail significant personal expense. And if that's true for one lost person, just imagine the combined tab when we start trying to reach whole families, communities, and countries!

Before we get all feverish about the concept of contagious Christianity, maybe we ought to slow down and do our own cost/benefit analysis in order to project how this enterprise will come out. Sound like a good idea?

Let's reverse the order. We'll start with the benefits and then spell out some costs. Next, we'll weigh the two sides and decide where we should go from there. If the price is too high, you can cash in this book for the latest John Grisham novel. But if it goes the other way, we'll roll up our sleeves and get busy. Fair enough?

Personal benefits of contagious Christianity

Adventure

This might surprise you. You've probably thought of communicating your faith as an important obligation, something you may feel guilty about not doing more. But until you really dive in, you won't realise that extending Christ to others can give your relationship with Him an exciting sense of the unexpected.

God gets great pleasure from sending His agents on secret reconnaissance missions with personal instructions no one else knows about. He loves to stretch us beyond our comfort zones and challenge us to take risks on the front lines of His Kingdom-advancement enterprises. He delights in giving us action-on-the-edge where, with white knuckles, we'll cling to Him as He takes us on the spiritual ride of our lives. The thrilling part is that He does this to help us grow as well as to spread His love to more and more wayward people.

In other words, the Christian life is one of faith, where we find ourselves routinely overdriving our headlights but knowing it's okay because God is in control and has a purpose behind it.

Before we get all feverish about the concept of contagious Christianity, maybe we ought to slow down and do our own cost/benefit analysis in order to project how this enterprise will come out. If the price is too high, you can cash in this book for the latest John Grisham novel.

Does this image excite you? If not, it might be a sign that you've been playing it safe in your spiritual life. Maybe it's time to take steps toward becoming a more contagious Christian, one God can use in His exciting search-and-rescue mission.

I know what it's like to have my spiritual life get stagnant, and then to see God open an opportunity to speak for Him. I rarely feel completely prepared, but it's always exhilarating when I open my mouth anyway and begin to sense that He's using me.

My trip to the health club was looking like just another mundane fifty-five minutes of laps and reps until my Indian Muslim friend walked up and poured his heart out to me. Suddenly I knew God had transformed an ordinary workout into an extraordinary faith-adventure.

A friend of mine was having a silencer put on his car not long ago. Needless to say, sitting in the customer waiting room was hardly the high-light of his week. But he decided to make the most of the time by looking over his workbook from our church's evangelism seminar that he'd recently completed.

"What's that you're reading?" a stranger suddenly asked. And just that fast, Dave's visit to the garage was transformed from a nuisance into a golden opportunity.

It was just another of numerous weekly flights for a commercial pilot who attends Willow Creek Community Church in the USA. There wasn't anything special about the night or unusual about the weather on this routine trip.

Nothing out of the ordinary—until he struck up a spiritual conversation with his co-pilot and, at 4:30 AM in the cockpit of a 727 at 28,000 feet, ended up leading him in a prayer of commitment to Christ! Now, *that's* adventure—even if they did pray with their eyes open!

Is your spiritual life lacking some action? Do you want to see God turn the routine into the remarkable? God is waiting to make it happen, and that's just one of the benefits of becoming a contagious Christian.

The Christian life is one of faith, where we find ourselves routinely overdriving our headlights but knowing it's okay because God is in control and has a purpose behind it.

Purpose

As you begin to experience more and more of the adventures God can create out of everyday situations, you'll find yourself facing daily tasks with a whole new sense of purpose. You'll start anticipating that He might surprise you at any time with an eternity-altering opportunity.

Trips to the health club, garage, or your workplace become, in your mind, thinly-veiled excursions into the realm of divine possibility. You'll start asking yourself, "Just what might God be up to in *this* situation?"

Part of the excitement of this perspective is that you may begin to see the hand of God even behind difficult events and circumstances.

Some time ago our church published its own magazine. In order to capture a story about a hospital we were helping, we sent our editor, Rob Wilkins, and our photographer, Larry Kayser, to Haiti. Their week went according to plan—until they got to the airport and boarded their homeward-bound six-seat chartered aeroplane.

Suddenly two soldiers who had been part of a failed coup attempt jumped the airport's security fence and stormed the small aircraft with machine guns and explosives in hand. As they forced their way aboard the plane, they demanded in broken English to be flown immediately to Miami.

It was a dangerous situation that could have ended in disaster. But Rob and Larry were able to view their predicament as something with divine purpose.

After their plane had taken off, they managed to ease tensions by asking these two frightened men about their families. Before they knew it, the weapons had been put away and they were sharing cans of Coke with them as they continued to talk and even laugh together. And if that isn't amazing enough, before the flight was over they had drawn a gospel illustration on a piece of paper in an effort to explain God's love and the forgiveness He offers through Christ.

To Rob and Larry, it didn't make much difference who these men were or what they had done. They still mattered to God, and they needed to know it. It was that awareness that put *purpose* into what was otherwise a difficult and dangerous situation.

It's incredible to realise that what we do each day has meaning in the big picture of God's plan.

Fulfilment

As we begin to throw ourselves into rescuing irreligious people and looking for purpose in everyday events, we start to feel a sense of fulfilment that transcends the realm of everyday human experience. What else could compare to being an instrument in God's hand, used to communicate His love and clarify His truth to people He cared enough to die for? There's nothing more satisfying than effectively furthering God's redemptive purpose for humanity!

What is that purpose? It's summed up in 2 Peter 3:9, which says, "He is patient with you, not wanting anyone to perish, but everyone to come to repentance." Jesus modelled this in John 4 when He talked with a wayward Samaritan by the side of a well.

We don't need to examine the whole interchange to see the fulfilment Jesus felt as a result of their brief encounter. When afterwards His disciples offered Him some food, He replied, "My food is to do the will of him who sent me and to finish his work . . . I tell you, open your eyes and look at the fields! They are ripe for harvest" (vv. 34–35).

In essence, He was saying, "I just played a part in fulfilling God's primary purpose of reaching this messed-up world—*and I eat that up!*" Really! Look at the verse again. He called this activity His "food". He did so because of the deeply satisfying feeling of fulfilment that comes when we contagiously spread our faith to other people.

Mark, the co-author of this book, attempted to communicate Christ to a fifty-seven-year-old Jewish man. You can imagine the time and energy he spent talking with a man who had been steeped in the Jewish faith and culture for so many years. But when Mark finally prayed with this man to embrace Jesus as his Messiah, you'd better believe he felt some major-league fulfilment. And when they met a year later to celebrate the one-year spiritual birthday of this man, who was now attending a seminary to prepare for full-time ministry, Mark could barely contain the joy he felt!

Spiritual growth

This is one of the most important, but often overlooked, benefits of contagious Christianity. Often I meet Christians who are in spiritual malaise, holding onto their faith but not advancing it much. Bible study has become a chore; prayer is a dry routine. The miracle of their own conversion, once recounted with great passion, is now a distant, fading memory. And going to church is—well, it's something they just *do*. Mechanically and half-heartedly, these people trudge along through the drudgery of quarantined Christianity.

But when these lethargic believers break out of spiritual isolation and meet some spiritual seekers, something incredible starts to happen. As they experience the high-stakes conversations that tend to happen with unchurched people, they begin to notice a sort of inner renewal taking place. Areas long ignored suddenly come alive with fresh significance.

Scripture reading, for example, becomes revitalised. They used to pull out the Bible once in a while, partly to see what they could learn from it and partly to alleviate some guilt. But now they've *got* to read it—even *memorise* parts of it—in order to know what they're talking about in the next exchange of spiritual ideas.

What's really exciting is that in addition to boning up for talking with others, they start to renew a genuine desire for fresh glimpses into God's character and truth. So what started as dutifully helping someone else changes into a personal desire for intimacy with God.

Similar changes happen in the area of prayer. Talking to God suddenly takes on new purpose. Stale recitations get displaced by impassioned pleas for the salvation of destruction-bound friends. And as spiritual progress is noticed in their lives, enthusiasm for prayer escalates all the more because there are now fresh reasons to thank Him, as well as critical concerns to bring His way.

And the benefits don't stop there. As we all know, the hardest part of prayer is getting started. But concern for our spiritually confused friends can jump-start us, and our conversations with God will spill over into all kinds of diverse areas. We find ourselves once again experiencing living and growing prayer lives!

Our desire to worship God grows, too. How could you *not* express gratitude to a God who so graciously and patiently extends His love to rebels like we were and like many of our friends still are? Naturally you start praising God for who He is and what He does, and before you know it you find you've again become a heart-driven worshipper.

What about personal purity? A benefit of becoming a contagious Christian is that it helps you maintain a high standard of conduct. You gain a heightened awareness that you're God's representative and that what you do really matters because it positively or negatively impacts the lives of others.

I know a man at our church who couldn't kick the

habit of excessive gambling at the local race track. After many frustrating rounds of quitting and starting again, he had reluctantly decided to just live with it. But then one of our staff members challenged him on it: not because it's the ultimate sin, but because it was hindering his ability to influence his friends for Christ.

With newfound motivation, this man gave up "playing the ponies" once and for all. Interestingly, he is now one of the most contagious Christians in our church!

Trips to the health club, garage, or your workplace become, in your mind, thinly-veiled excursions into the realm of divine possibility. You'll start asking yourself, "Just what might God be up to in this situation?"

There's another important aspect to this area of personal purity: When you start going on record with those around you that you're a serious Christian, they begin immediately and instinctively to watch your life. Some do it out of curiosity, others out of a desire to find fault. Either way, it provides a highly effective system of accountability. Your irreligious friends actually assist you in becoming a more godly man or woman. What an added bonus to our list of personal benefits!

The last item on our spiritual growth list is church attendance. Having a heightened sense of concern for lost people will affect our participation in two ways. First, it will motivate us to take advantage of all that our church offers to help us grow in spiritual strength and stamina. Second, it will provoke us to make changes in our churches in areas that may have become outdated, inefficient, or even counterproductive. We begin to realise that the task of the church is too important to let it run on fewer than eight cylinders. So with fresh motivation, we can start helping the church become all it was meant to be in order to reach irreligious people and turn them into fully devoted followers of Christ.

Isn't it incredible how elevating our efforts to reach others can be a catalyst for personal growth? But in case that's not enough, here are a few other benefits.

Spiritual confidence

Engaging in efforts to extend your faith to others can go a long way toward strengthening your confidence in your own beliefs. This is true, in part, because talking to people who have different spiritual perspectives will force you to take steps to ensure you are speaking accurately about the Christian faith.

It's similar to going to university and taking the final exam at the end of the course. Preparing for that exam forces you to exercise your memory and intensify your study habits in order to show the professor—and yourself—how much you know. What's ironic is that the act of preparing to show others what we know is often what causes us for the first time to understand it clearly ourselves.

We automatically increase our own knowledge when we try to communicate our faith to friends who are sceptics, or Mormons, or Jehovah's Witnesses, or New Agers, or even church-going non-Christians. And when we successfully hold our own in the face of opposition, we gain a heightened sense of spiritual confidence.

And if you think that builds your self-assurance, imagine what happens when one of these people becomes a Christian. Your faith is boosted sky high! You may feel like seeking out some Muslim fundamentalists or hardened atheists. Why not? They matter to God, too.

There's no telling who He'll use you to reach, once your spiritual confidence starts spiralling upward!

Enduring investments

Jesus warned his followers not to "store up for yourselves treasures on earth, where moth and rust destroy, and where thieves break in and steal. But store up for yourselves treasures in heaven, where moth and rust do not destroy, and where thieves do not break in and steal" (Matthew 6:19–20). Peter used even stronger terms: "But the day of the Lord will come like a thief. The heavens will disappear with a roar; the elements will be destroyed by fire, and the earth and everything in it will be laid bare. Since everything will be destroyed in this way, what kind of people ought you to be?" (2 Peter 3:10–11).

Let me ask this: How better could you expend your time and energy than investing it in people, many of whom will thank you for all of eternity in heaven? What other investment will reap so high a reward?

I'll never forget the force with which that passage hit me when I first read it many years ago. I had been a casual Christian, caught up in the pursuit of trinkets, toys, and earthly pleasures. I even remember thinking, "This is amazing! I can have all of this and heaven, too!"

And then this Scripture knocked the wind out of my sails. As its truth began to transform my values, a friend made an interesting suggestion. He said I should get a bunch of red stickers, write on them, "Soon To Be

Burned", and put them on everything I owned! It would serve as a constant reminder that every car, every motorcycle, every boat, every piece of furniture—everything I had or wanted—is subject to rust, decay, and theft, and will ultimately be destroyed in a great fiery blaze.

What a future! And what a mistake to invest so much time and energy in things that won't last. Though I never actually put stickers on my possessions, I'm thankful God helped me start understanding this critical lesson so many years ago. It prompted me to make the decision to orient my life around the only things that *do* last: God, His Kingdom, and people like you, me, and those we'll reach for Him. These alone are worthy of our central passion.

The honour of being God's agent

When we realise how great God is and how weak and dependent we are, the words of Jesus in Acts 1:8 become almost incomprehensible: "You will receive power when the Holy Spirit comes on you; and you will be my witnesses in Jerusalem, and in all Judea and Samaria, and to the ends of the earth."

Can't you see the disciples turning and looking behind themselves to see who He was talking to? I can imagine them saying, "Who, *us*? Lord, you've *got* to be kidding! We were just getting used to the fact that You came back to life, and now You're going to take off and leave this whole Kingdom-expansion project to *us*? This is *incredible*!"

And it's no less amazing—or true—today than it was then. Hard as it is to grasp, God has chosen us to be His agents. He's given us the high honour of speaking on His behalf. And He promises to empower and use us in the process.

I'll never forget one of the first times this really hit home for me. It was during my early ministry days when

I was working with high school students. We had planned a big Wednesday night outreach event, and all of our members worked hard to invite their friends to hear the gospel message, perhaps for the first time.

The night came, the place was full, and it was almost time for me to step up to the podium. I remember feeling an extreme case of "the ordinaries". Maybe this happens to you, too. You start thinking things like, "Who am *I* to be getting up there talking to all these kids? I barely know this stuff myself, so what makes me think I can convey anything meaningful to them?"

Can you relate to those feelings? Even now, after many years of ministry, I often get hit with a wave of the ordinaries. But it helps me to remember that it was *God* who bestowed upon us the high honour of being His representatives. It wasn't our idea! So while we need to pray and prepare, in a very real sense what happens from there is *His* problem. And as I found out that night so long ago, it's a problem He loves to solve in order to show His power by doing the extraordinary through us.

In spite of my self-doubt, and knees that were literally shaking, I got up and explained to these students to the best of my limited abilities that they mattered to God. And I told them it wasn't enough for them to believe God loved them, but that they also needed to come to Christ to receive His forgiveness and leadership. And when I asked them to take that step, I was amazed to see several hundred students stand to their feet!

In fact, I was so startled that I thought they'd misunderstood me. So I told them to sit back down so I could re-explain the gospel and the kind of commitment I was talking about. And then, even *more* of them stood to their feet!

Beyond my wildest dreams, God had honoured the feeble efforts of one of his apprentice ambassadors as He altered the eternities of scores of high school students. I remember afterward walking behind the building we had met in, leaning against a wall, and being overwhelmed with feelings of gratitude and amazement that He would use someone the likes of me.

And guess what? He can use someone the likes of *you*, too. It might not be in front of high school students, but perhaps over a fence, a desk, a table at a restaurant, at a construction site, a squash court, or a podium. God has bestowed on you the honour of being His spokesperson. He has promised that He'll honour your efforts to become a contagious Christian by rewarding you and touching others.

The closer you look, the more you see that the rewards are high and the costs relatively low, especially when we understand that ultimately they're not costs at all. They're investments that pay permanent dividends.

Are those enough personal benefits to whet your appetite? We haven't even talked about all that the recipients of our efforts will gain. You know, little stuff, like escaping the prospect of hell and gaining the promise of heaven, not to mention having a life here on earth filled with adventure, purpose, fulfilment, growth, spiritual confidence, lasting investments, and the honour of becoming agents for the God of the universe!

On top of that, God benefits, too. He has the reward of watching His children emulate His love for lost people, a kind of joy any parent can readily understand. John 15:8 says, "This is to my Father's glory, that you bear much fruit. . . ." In addition, remember that when we are successful in leading someone to faith, Luke 15:10 tells us that "there is rejoicing in the presence of the angels of God over one sinner who repents." It's a celestial celebration!

So when we become active and strategic in trying to reach people for Christ, when we become more contagious in the way we live and express our faith, we find that we benefit, others benefit, and even God benefits.

But one question remains. Just what is the cost of this kind of personal outreach, and does it offset our extensive list of benefits?

The costs of contagious Christianity

Time and energy

You know and I know that reaching wayward people will not be easy. It will involve the expending of time and energy, our most valued resources, in order to build relationships, showing Christian care and compassion, and praying consistently. It will involve explaining and re-explaining the seemingly simple gospel message, waiting patiently while they "think about it" (knowing that in many cases they're really running from it), trying to cope with a myriad of challenging questions, and, in the back of your mind, realising that they might end up rejecting Christ. It sounds like a formula for frustration, doesn't it?

But let me ask this: How better could you expend your time and energy than investing it in people, many of whom will thank you for all of eternity in heaven? What other investment will reap so high a reward?

Reading and study

In order to reach others, it's going to take some Bible study and, occasionally, reading books like this one. But is this really so bad? Sure, it takes some effort to make certain you know what you're talking about, but you'd want to be up on what you believe anyway, wouldn't you? Scripture tells all of us to keep growing in our knowledge and understanding of God. Besides, it's not fair to list Bible study on the cost side of the equation when we've already listed it on the benefit side!

Money

It's true that investing in the lives of others takes a tangible investment. Lunches, long-distance phone calls (a friend of mine once made a three-and-a-half-hour long-distance call to share his faith with someone he knew, and she later came to Christ), the cost of books, seminars, and the sometimes high expense of providing for the physical needs of others—these are some of the financial demands contagious Christianity can have on our wallets.

But when tha bill is totalled, the amount of hard cash spent is usually still relatively low, especially in comparison to the overwhelming rewards that result. And for those situations where the cost is higher, these words of Jesus offer appropriate encouragement: "Store up for yourselves treasures in heaven, where moth and rust do not destroy, and where thieves do not break in and steal. For where your treasure is, there your heart will be also" (Matthew 6:20–21). I can't imagine a safer investment, can you?

Risk of embarrassment, rejection, or persecution

While probably few of us suffer overt persecution, the likelihood is high that we'll experience some lesser kinds of resistance. It could be teasing from friends, or just the lonely feeling of being left out of certain conversations or social gatherings. But it can also get more serious when there's discrimination or intentional harassment because of what we represent.

I don't have any easy answers. I would only encourage you to ask God for His vantage point as you look at the benefits of obeying Him. He offers comfort through verses like, "Blessed are you when people insult you, persecute you and falsely say all kinds of evil against you because of me. Rejoice and be glad, because great is your reward in heaven" (Matthew 5:11–12), and "Let us not become weary in doing good, for at the proper time we will reap a harvest if we do not give up" (Galatians 6:9).

It complicates your life

For most of us, the primary cost of reaching others is that it entangles us in the concerns and activities of their lives. It encroaches upon our independence. It adds details to our overloaded schedules. Simply stated, it complicates our already complicated lives.

But so does getting married. And having children. And buying a house. And, for that matter, becoming a Christian. Think about it. All of these areas require time, effort, learning, some risk and, without question, a fair share of money. Most of the things that are important complicate our lives. But are they worth it? Of course they are!

Ask any new mother whether her baby requires time and energy, and she'll probably dare you to try keeping pace with her for just one day and night! When she's not feeding, holding, or bathing her baby, you'll probably find her reading books about parenting, because the learning process never ends. And don't even bring up the subject of money! She'll drag out bills to show you the high cost of everything from formula to baby grows. "Have you seen the cost of nappies lately?" she'd say.

But then inquire whether, in light of all these costs,

she regrets having the baby. "Are you crazy?" she'd ask. "Having this baby has been one of the highlights of my life. I *love* this baby!"

The outcome

It's safe to say that we can conclude the same about becoming a contagious Christian. Just review the lists! Sure, there are costs, efforts, risks, and complications involved, but it's worth it—a thousandfold. The closer you look, the more you see that the rewards are high and the costs relatively low, especially when we understand that ultimately they're not costs at all. *They're investments that pay permanent dividends.*

I don't know about you, but when I see the way the scales tip decisively in our cost/benefit analysis, it excites me to get on with the adventure at hand: Namely, how can we take steps toward heightening our contagiousness and begin to experience all the rewards God has for us? That's the subject we'll explore in the next chapter.

CHAPTER THREE

A Formula for Impacting Your World

One of the most frustrating experiences in life is to be told what to do without being given a clear idea of how to go about doing it. Unfortunately, this kind of thing happens all the time.

Your boss sets a sky-high sales quota and lets you know in no uncertain terms that he expects you to meet it. He informs you that overall revenue must be raised, costs lowered, and the bottom line improved, but how you get it all done is *your* problem.

Or your teacher barks out more and more assignments as the books and homework pile up, and the frustration grows. Read this, write that, work it out, turn it in, take the exam, pass the course. And the professor seems unconcerned that you have four other classes with equally high demands. You'll just have to work it out somehow, but how you do it is a test you'll have to take alone. No wonder so many of us have frequent nightmares about uncompleted classes!

Even in church we're bombarded with expectations to have strong marriages, obedient children, balanced budgets, ethical businesses, effective prayer lives and meaningful relationships. But while the "ought to" comes through loudly and clearly, the "how to" often remains distant and muffled, if it's heard at all.

One place where this is especially true is in the challenge to have an evangelistic impact on your world. "People are lost," the preacher exclaims. "They're headed for hell, God wants to reach them, and you're His chosen ambassador—so you'd better get out there and bring them to Christ!"

How can you argue with that? It's biblical, it rings true, and it makes sense. So here I go to take some action on it—but where? Could somebody elaborate on that technical term "get out there"? How do I get started? What does the process look like? Who'll help me take the first step?

A divine plan

Thank God He didn't leave us in such a state of confusion. There's an old saying, "What God expects, He enables." Not only does He tells us that this world of wayward people matters to Him, but He also sees to it that we have the information we need to start us on the path of effectively reaching them.

Jesus talked about His plan for doing this a long time ago when He sat with His followers on the side of a hill near Capernaum. Using everyday terms, He explained principles that can be boiled down to this precise plan for influencing our world:

$$HP + CP + CC = MI$$

What does this cryptic equation mean? While it may look like something out of a chemistry textbook, it's actually a formula that contains God's strategy for reaching spiritually lost people.

We'll break with standard algebra and start right off with the last element, MI. That means *Maximum*

Impact: to have the greatest spiritual influence possible on those around us. This is God's purpose, expressed throughout the Bible.

As we've seen, Acts 1:8 tells us we are to be His witnesses, empowered by His Spirit to reach people near and far. Second Corinthians 5:19 says that when we've been reconciled with God through Christ, we are given the ministry of helping sinful men and women come to peace with God. Matthew 28:19–20, often referred to as The Great Commission, tells us to go into the whole world, spread the gospel message, lead people to Christ and then baptise and build them up in the faith. Elsewhere Jesus says we are to be fishers of men.

You see, the Scriptures are brimming with challenges to each of us to arrange our lives so that we can have the highest possible spiritual influence on those around us. It's our responsibility to put those challenges into action; it's His to produce results by drawing people to Himself.

Before we explore the rest of our formula's component parts, we need to examine its source. It flows out of two elements Jesus used as illustrations: Salt and Light.

It was in the middle of the greatest sermon in history, the Sermon on the Mount, that Jesus said these famous words: "You are the salt of the earth . . . you are the light of the world." He wanted all of His followers to see themselves as salt and light in how they lived out their lives in the world.

A new view of salt

Let's look at the first one. Why would Jesus use a metaphor like salt? What does salt do? These days, it makes us nervous because it can lead to high blood pressure. So we feel guilty every time we reach for the shaker. But let's look across the spans of time and think about the primary uses of salt throughout history.

The first thing that comes to mind is that salt makes us thirsty. That's why bars in America serve salty pretzels and peanuts free of charge, to get people to drink more. Or so I'm told!

Salt does something else, too: It spices things up. Who does this? Can it be ommited? When we eat something that tastes a little bland we reflexively reach for the salt in order to enhance the flavour.

And salt preserves. We don't use it for this purpose much anymore, but before the days of the refrigerator, salt was widely used to prevent foods from spoiling. Certain meats could be preserved for long periods of time if they were carefully packed in salt.

So salt stimulates thirst, it adds excitement to the taste of things, and it holds back decay. Which leads us to the big question: Which of these did Jesus have in mind when He looked at His followers and said, "You are the salt of the earth"?

"What God expects, He enables." Not only does He tell us that this world of wayward people matters to Him, but He also sees to it that we have the information we need to start us on the path of effectively reaching them.

The short answer is, *we don't know*! How's that for candour? If you read the scholars on this question, using poker parlance, they'll hold the three cards and say, "Pick a card, any card. Or all three cards, if you'd like."

It could be that Jesus meant for salt to symbolise the idea of creating thirst. When Christians are in tune with the Holy Spirit, and when they live in their world with a sense of purpose, and with peace and joy, this often creates a spiritual thirst in the people around them.

At Willow Creek, in America, we often hear testimonies about this. People say things like, "I was at work, and I noticed someone in my department who lived a little differently and talked a bit differently and valued some things differently. It caught my interest. I sensed a growing spiritual thirst inside of me that I'd never experienced before."

When Christians live out their faith with authenticity and boldness they put a little zing into a sometimes bland cup of soup. They catch people off-guard and make them wince. They wake people up with their challenges and seemingly radical points of view. And they overturn a few applecarts here and there. In short, they put some spice into the lives of those around them.

What's more, when believers are living Christ-honouring lives they hold back the moral decay in society. I hope that's what's happening with the abortion dilemma, with environmental concerns, with racism, and with the breakdown of the family. As Christians honour God, He uses them to stem the tidal wave of evil that's threatening to sweep the land.

So pick a card—any card. Any or all three might be exactly what Jesus had in mind when He used the word salt. But upon further reflection you might discover additional reasons Jesus chose the salt metaphor, reasons that can be easily overlooked.

First, in order for salt to have the greatest possible impact, it must be potent enough to have an effect. And second, for any impact to take place, salt has to get close to whatever it's supposed to affect. So Jesus may have chosen the salt metaphor because salt requires both *potency* and *proximity* to do its thing.

That leads us back to the formula:

HP + CP + CC = MI

Having established that the end purpose of the formula is to produce *Maximum Impact*, we can now move to the front and look at the first two elements needed to reach that goal: HP + CP. HP means *High Potency*, and CP, *Close Proximity*.

That's exactly what we need as Christians if we're going to influence people who are outside the family of God. We must have high potency, which means a strong enough concentration of Christ's influence in our lives that His power and presence will be undeniable to others. And we've got to have plenty of proximity. We need to get close to people we're hoping to reach in order to allow His power to have its intended effect.

In Matthew 5:13 Jesus said that salt that is without savour and of inferior quality is worthless. It has lost its power. It won't create much thirst, won't add much spice, won't retard much decay. It can have all kinds of proximity—it can be poured all over something we want it to affect—but if it lacks potency it is, Jesus said, useless. About all it does is give people something to stomp on.

By the same token, highly flavoured, industrial-strength salt has great potency, but it can't produce any results unless it touches something. As Becky Pippert wrote many years ago, unless salt gets poured out of the shaker, it remains a mere table ornament.

That, unfortunately, is a fairly good description of a lot of people who call themselves Christians. Oh, they've got a lot of potency in their own relationship with Christ. They walk a God-honouring path in their personal patterns of living. But they never get out where they can rub up next to people who need their influence. They're good-looking table ornaments, but they have low impact.

Do you see why Jesus' choice of the salt metaphor was so compelling? With it He was able to show that both components—potency and proximity—have to be employed before we can fulfil our mission to have a spiritual impact on our family and friends.

When Christians live out their faith with authenticity and boldness they put a little zing into a sometimes bland cup of soup. They catch people off-guard and make them wince. They wake people up with their challenges and seemingly radical points of view. And they overturn a few applecarts here and there.

A powerful example

A few years ago my wife and I spent a day with Billy and Ruth Graham at their mountaintop home in North Carolina. In the evening I could tell Billy was starting to get tired, so I told him we were going to head back to our hotel. But to my surprise he handed me his Bible and said, "Bill, before you go, feed me from God's word."

I thought to myself, this seventy-three-year-old man is obviously *not* a baby Christian. And there's no savour problem here, either! In addition, he has communicated the gospel message to more people than anyone else in history. Yet here he was saying to me, in effect, "I still need and love to be fed from God's Word."

This experience helped me understand why Billy Graham has maintained such a high-potency factor for so long. He continually takes steps to heighten his saltiness. Nothing that happened during our time together lingered with me more than that did. I left, hoping that my savour factor will be sky high when I'm that age. I would like to be *dangerous* when I'm seventy-three—wouldn't you?

How is that going to happen? It'll happen when we take the steps that make us highly potent at age eighteen, and thirty-eight, and fifty-eight. What are they? I wish I could offer you a spine-tingling, bungy-jumping kind of answer, but I can't. It comes, rather, by practicing the age-old daily spiritual disciplines that have made believers salty for thousands of years, and there's nothing fancy or high-tech about it.

When it comes to developing and maintaining high potency, there's no magic wand and there are no shortcuts. Our savour factor will be roughly proportionate to the extent to which we engage in the age-old spiritual disciplines.

High potency comes from reading and feeding on the truths of the Bible. It comes from being on our knees in prayer. It comes from rubbing shoulders with other contagious Christians in small group fellowships, where brothers and sisters in Christ attempt to take the masks off and be real with each other. It comes from serving and contributing in a biblically functioning church. It comes from trying to actively share your faith with others, and experiencing both successes and failures along the way. It comes from disciplining ourselves for the purpose of sustained saltiness.

When it comes to developing and maintaining high

potency, there's no magic wand and there are no short-cuts. Our savour factor will be roughly proportionate to the extent to which we engage in the age-old spiritual disciplines. Daily contact with God and His Word will keep us open to the Spirit's leadings, eager to influence people outside the family, loving and tender before God and each other, and tuned into what's really important.

These activites will not only keep us tapped into God's divine power, they will also help us develop the traits of a contagious Christian, which we'll discuss in the next section.

There aren't many Billy Grahams around, but we can all take steps to raise our understanding of what it takes to have high potency. Undoubtedly, each of us has room to grow in character and in connectedness to God so as to become stronger salt. The way you live your life can create thirst, add spice, and serve as a moral preservative as you interact with those around you.

A lesson from light

As we saw earlier, salt was just one of two metaphors Jesus used in describing what His followers should be like. The other was light. He said in Matthew 5:14, "You are the light of the world." It is again appropriate to ask what made Jesus choose this metaphor. What does light do?

The most basic answer is that it makes things visible and helps us see them for what they really are. It's what we mean when we say we want to "shed some light" on an issue.

And when we look into the biblical use of the term "light", the central idea that emerges is that of clearly and attractively presenting God's truth to others, *illuminating* it in order to show it for what it really is. And while the metaphor includes the need to model a lifestyle that will stand in contrast to the drabness of life without Christ, the distinctive idea seems to be that of lucidly articulating the content of the gospel message.

This can be seen in other Scripture passages that refer to light. For example, in 2 Corinthians 4:5–6 we're told that when the message of Christ was first clarified to us, God "made his light shine in our hearts to give us *the light of the knowledge of the glory of God* in the face of Christ." Do you see the link between light and the conveying of information about the gospel message?

Similarly, in the Matthew passage, Jesus seems to be saying He wants His followers to be able to spiritually illuminate others not only by living out His teachings, but also by explaining His message of forgiveness and grace with precision and accuracy. That's what it is to be light.

So just as the salt illustration gave us the first two components of our formula, HP (high potency) + CP (close proximity), so now the light metaphor provides the final component of our formula for having maximum impact on others. It is CC, which stands for *Clear Communication* of the gospel message. Putting it all together, we get:

HP + CP (salt) + CC (light) = MI

For light to have its intended effect, Jesus says in Matthew 5:15–16, it must not be covered up or obscured in any way. And in order for us to have the powerful influence God desires, we must know the gospel message thoroughly and be ready to communicate it concisely and clearly.

This implies that we'll have to do some extra work to learn how to declare and defend the major tenets of the gospel with straightforward simplicity. We need to be ready to help people understand God's nature, their sinfulness, Christ's payment, and the step each of us must take to receive the forgiveness and new life He offers.

Without this, people are left guessing what it is that sets us apart in our quality of living. They may doubt that they could ever experience the kind of transformed life they see in us.

So can we just come out and say it? Far too many Christians have been anaesthetised into thinking that if they simply live out their faith in an open and consistent fashion, the people around them will see it, want it, and somehow figure out how to get it for themselves. Or they reason that maybe these people will come and ask them what makes their life so special and, when they do, they'll seize the opportunity and explain it to them. But let's be honest: That almost never happens.

While it's a prerequisite to live a salty Christian life—to be highly potent and in relationship with others—that alone is not enough. God forbid that we stop there, because people end up in hell on that plan. It's imperative that we also put the message into clear language our friends can understand and act upon.

Paul asks in Romans 10:14, "How can they believe in the one of whom they have not heard? And how can they hear without someone preaching to them?" Jesus said we should not only be salt, but also light: clearly communicating His message of grace. If we're both, we'll enable the people we care about to do what He says in Matthew 5:16. After they've had an opportunity to "see your good deeds" and understand the central gospel message, they'll be ready to make a decision to follow Christ and meaningfully "praise your Father in heaven."

Making an honest assessment

So let's pause to ask the big question. Does this equation accurately describe the current condition of your own life? Take a look at it one more time while you think about this important question.

HP/high potency + CP/close proximity + CC/clear communication = MI/maximum impact

I know many people for whom this is an accurate description. I marvel at the degree of savour in their spiritual lives. And I'm thrilled to see the lengths to which they'll go to rub shoulders with irreligious people in order to influence them for Christ. These people inspire and challenge me.

But many other Christians are flirting with funny arithmetic. They're trying to get that "new math" to work. They say, "I'm going to figure out a way to make high potency and *low* proximity add up to maximum impact." But they can't succeed, because they remain isolated from the very people they need to touch.

Far too many Christians have been anaesthetised into thinking that if they simply live out their faith in an open and consistent fashion, the people around them will see it, want it, and somehow figure out how to get it for themselves.

Others say, "I'll have all the proximity you can imagine. I'll run with those crowds so much that I'll become *indistinguishable*! And then I'll have maximum impact." No you won't—not until you have distinctiveness, potency, and savour.

Many more people try to conclude the matter by saying, "Okay, I'll get my savour factor up high by living a consistent Christian life, and then I'll exert the needed efforts to get into influence-range with the people I'd like to reach. But please don't ask me to actually *say* anything! I'll just live out my faith in front of them and maybe some of it will begin to rub off."

As time will prove, however, that's only wishful thinking. Just as words without actions are futile, actions without words are devoid of meaning and content. Can you see why Jesus emphasised that we need to be both salt *and* light? It's critical that we have a high savour factor *and* a readiness to articulate the message of Christ.

A sneak preview

Given that our goal is to have the highest spiritual influence possible, it's important that we explore these topics more fully in order to shore up each ingredient in the equation. That's what we'll do for the remainder of this book.

If we're to have any hope of attracting people to Christ, we'll have to fulfil the first part of the formula by developing some critically important character traits like authenticity, compassion, and sacrifice. These will be explored in the next three chapters, which make up a unit called, "The Prerequisite of High Potency".

Next, we'll expand on the second element in the equation in the section called, "The Potential of Close Proximity". There we'll discuss practical ways we can naturally move into influence-range with others. We'll explore the everyday opportunities for spiritual impact that awaits us in ordinary relationships, many of which we already have. This is where the adventure really begins!

For example, recently I was getting a haircut and noticed that the stylist was in a bad mood. I wanted to try to cheer her up a bit, but I couldn't figure out a way to start a conversation. Then I noticed a song that was playing on their sound system. It featured a saxophone, so I decided to take a shot in the dark. Casually, I said, "That's Kenny G, isn't it?" She replied with great enthusiasm, "I *love* Kenny G! Do *you* know Kenny G?"

Jesus isn't like the boss, the teacher, or the preacher who just gives us our assignment and then leaves us to figure out how to do it on our own. He gave us the formula, and then He bet the redemptive farm on it.

Parenthetically, you need to understand something. I was way out on a limb at this point. I think I've seen a total of about fifteen seconds of Kenny G on television. All I remember is that he played with his mouthpiece over on the side of his mouth. It made me want to slide way to the end of the couch to watch him. I was just glad she didn't ask me if I knew what the "G" in his name stood for, because I had no idea!

After we had talked a while about Kenny G's music, the conversation gradually came around to more significant matters, including her personal life. She told me she was a single parent, so we talked about what had happened to her marriage and how her kids were coping with the changes.

"They're handling it pretty well," she said, "because they get a lot of help from a church in the area called Willow Creek."

"That's interesting," I said, trying to contain my enthusiasm.

I asked if she'd ever gone herself and she told me she had, a long time earlier. When I asked her why she had stopped going she said she didn't know. So I told her I'd heard that the church had an amnesty week coming up—no matter what you've done or why you left, you can come back, no questions asked! She looked at me somewhat quizzically and said, "Are you serious?" I replied, "Yeah, sort of," since that would be true at Willow Creek *any* week!

I don't know whether she has come back to church yet or not, but I had a clear sense that God was pleased with the effort and might just use it to further His influence in her life. He loves it when we get in close proximity to people who desperately need Him. He enjoys it when we take risks in conversations and turn them from the mundane to topics that really matter. He finds joy in using ordinary Christians like you and me to spiritually affect others at close range.

But if that's going to happen, we'll have to learn to shine brighter. So the fourth section is called, "The Power of Clear Communication". This will be a critically important unit because the need for articulating the gospel is so high and the confidence level of many Christians is so low. Even if you've been spreading the faith for a long time, it is helpful to keep reviewing and practicing how to verbalise the message. If you don't, you'll get rusty. And if that happens, you'll find yourself instinctively side-stepping opportunities to raise spiritual topics of conversation because you won't feel ready to run with them.

The Bible says in Hosea 4:6 that "people are destroyed from lack of knowledge." The spiritual seeker in Acts 8:31 said in reference to the Scripture passage he was reading, "How can I [understand], unless someone explains it to me?' God has given you and me the charge to clarify His message to people throughout the world. The section on clear communication is designed to help you begin to do that in a way that is both natural and effective.

My treatment of this topic wouldn't be complete without the final section, "The Payoff: Maximum Impact". It will explain how you can personally usher someone across the line of faith into a relationship with Christ. This section also paints a picture of what a church can look like as more and more of its members apply this formula and become increasingly contagious.

It's exciting to know that this enterprise is central to God's purposes, and that we can be key players for Him as, together, we impact this world for eternity. I don't know about you, but that excites me!

How is it going to happen? After many years of hearing numerous leaders of large ministries present grandiose plans for how we can "reach our nation" or "change our world", or claim that "we're right on the verge of a spiritual revolution that will soon sweep our land," I've become more than a bit sceptical. And I'll bet you have, too.

Isn't it good to know that two thousand years ago Jesus sat on the side of a hill looking out over the sparkling waters of the Sea of Galilee and gave us a formula for changing our world? It involves two people: a salty Christian and someone who needs to come to faith, talking together about things that really matter.

Jesus isn't like the boss, the teacher, or the preacher who just gives us our assignment and then leaves us to figure out how to do it on our own. He gave us the formula, and then He bet the redemptive farm on it. Wherever there's high savour, close interaction, and a straightforward presentation of truth, and where the Holy Spirit is active, there is contagious Christian influence that might lead, eventually, to the salvation of one more lost person who matters deeply to God.

"You are the salt of the earth," Jesus said. "You are the light of the world." He meant *you*.

SECTION TWO

The Prerequisite of High Potency

HP **+ CP + CC = MI**

CHAPTER FOUR

The Attractiveness of Authenticity

"Image is Everything."

That's what a popular television advertising campaign told us, and apparently a lot of people believed it, especially church-goers. After all, look at how much energy is spent by individual believers and ministries to keep up a good front, even when deep conflicts and inconsistencies lurk below the surface.

Ironically, however, the motto of many sincere truth seekers is, "*Substance* is Everything." And these people can tell the difference a mile away. They have an uncanny ability to sniff out what is real and what isn't, and what they smell determines whether they're going to be attracted or repelled.

Lee Strobel was a reporter for the *Chicago Tribune* who began attending Willow Creek in the early '80s in an effort to appease his newly converted wife, Leslie. In his insightful book, *Inside the Mind of Unchurched Harry and Mary*, Lee recalls: "When I walked into church as a sceptical unbeliever, my 'hypocrisy antenna' was scanning the place for signs that people were just playing church. In fact, I was aggressively on the lookout for phoniness, opportunism, or deception, because I felt that if I could find an excuse for rejecting the church on grounds of hypocrisy, I could feel free to reject Christianity as well."

It turned out that Lee discovered the opposite. He found the church to be filled with people who were sincere in their efforts to figure out what it means to please and follow Christ in their daily lives. And it impacted him over time to the degree that he not only turned from his atheism to receive God's forgiveness, but he even committed his life to full-time ministry. Today he's one of Willow Creek's teaching pastors.

Inauthenticity among the ranks of those claiming to be Christians can become an almost insurmountable barrier to belief. This problem was summed up a few years ago in a song called "Jacob's Ladder", which topped the pop music charts. Huey Lewis sang about being pursued by a fat man who was selling salvation. It's not too surprising that he responded by saying he was not in a hurry to think about such things and then added scathingly, *"and I don't want to be like you."*

Most people won't come right out and say it, but you'd better believe they're thinking it. They're not interested in committing their lives to Christ unless they observe attractive and consistent patterns of living in the Christians they know. Joe Aldrich, author of the book, *Life-Style Evangelism*, puts it like this: "Christians are to *be* good news before they *share* the good news."

Jesus said, "If a man remains in me and I in him, he will bear much fruit" (John 15:5).

First things first

Though it's tempting, to run ahead and talk about practical tips for communicating our faith would be premature. You see, before we can become highly contagious Christians, we must first live in a way that convinces the people around us that we actually have the disease ourselves!

Inauthenticity among the ranks of those claiming to be Christians can become an almost insurmountable barrier to belief.

If we want to be the kind of high-impact, salty Christians that Jesus said we need to be, we're going to have to first take some preliminary steps of self-examination and then be willing to make any needed character adjustments. We must start by making certain that the way we're living backs up the words we're speaking. To modify those song lyrics, we want people to observe our lives and think to themselves, "I didn't think I'd ever feel such urgency about spiritual matters, *but I sure wish I could be like them*!"

So the natural question is this: How are Christians doing overall? To try to get an answer, I sometimes strike up casual conversations with people who don't know what I do for a living. "I'm curious," I'll say. "Do you know any Christians? And, if you do, what are they like? What general impressions do you have about them?"

Boy, do I get an earful! You ought to try it sometime. Far more frequently than I wish to admit, people produce some unsettling answers. They'll say, "I know some Christians and, well, I'd have to describe them as sort of uptight and narrow. You know—really rigid types." Others will say, "They're sort of isolated. They keep to themselves. I don't know them well because they're in their own world."

Other reports are worse: "I know some bornagainers, and I've got to tell you, they really bother me. I feel like I'm being condemned every time I walk by them. They're just too self-righteous." Or, "They're so simplistic, rattling off trite Bible answers for every complex problem." And, occasionally, "I think they're mostly a bunch of hypocrites."

What I've found both interesting and disappointing is how few of those outside the faith ever respond positively about Christians. I wish that whenever I'd ask people for their perceptions, the first thing out of their mouth would be something like: "Christians? They're people with integrity and moral courage." Or, "They're so filled with compassion. They're kind to others, especially those less fortunate than them." Or, "Christians tell the truth; you can count on them to shoot straight with you." Don't you wish the overall perception of what true believers are like was different from what many people carry around in their minds? We need better press, because the impressions people have of us will have a profound effect on how they view God.

Divine insight

Jesus knew the importance of perceptions. That's why He gave us such clear instructions about being salt and light. He knows that as you learn to live out these guidelines in tangible ways, people will begin to "see your good deeds and praise your Father in heaven."

Do you see what Jesus was getting at in these verses in Matthew 5? He was telling us that the attitudes and actions of each of His followers would either draw people toward a relationship with God or push them further away. So Jesus was pleading with His people—then and now—to live in a way that would draw people toward the Father. Think about it; how we conduct our daily lives has implications that reach all the way into eternity.

Recently I saw a letter written by a relatively new Christian to the person whose life had influenced hers so greatly. She actually lists about a dozen qualities she found contagious in the life of this older Christian. Listen to some of what she wrote:

> You know, when we met, I began to discover a new vulnerability, a warmth and a lack of pretense that impressed me. I saw in you a thriving spirit—no signs of internal stagnation anywhere. I could tell you were a growing person and I liked that. I saw you had strong self-esteem, not based on the fluff of self-help books, but on something a whole lot deeper. I saw that you lived by convictions and priorities and not just by convenience, selfish pleasure, and financial gain. And I had never met anyone like that before.
>
> I felt a depth of love and concern as you listened to me and didn't judge me. You tried to understand me, you sympathized and you celebrated with me, you demonstrated kindness and generosity—and not just to me, but to other people, as well.
>
> And you stood for something. You were willing to go against the grain of society and follow what you believed to be true, no matter what people said, and no matter how much it cost you. And for those reasons and a whole host of others, I found myself really wanting what you had. Now that I've become a Christian, I wanted to write to tell you I'm grateful beyond words for how you lived out your Christian life in front of me.

Basically, she was saying, "Thanks for being a contagious Christian." Reading a letter like that motivates me to live as a contagious Christian, too. How about you? I'll bet you want your life to count for a whole lot more than trinkets and toys and zeros on a paycheque, too.

Because this area is so critically important, we're going to spend three chapters focusing on some of the key qualities that encourage spiritually sensitive people to consider Christianity for themselves. Though others could be discussed, it is these three characteristics—authenticity, compassion, and sacrifice—that seem to be necessary for any Christian to be contagious. Remove them, and the seeker will almost assuredly look elsewhere. Live them out, and you'll become highly infectious in your influence on others.

The elements of authenticity

When teaching in smaller settings I've sometimes asked those in the group what qualities in other people bother them most. Do you know what almost always winds up at the top of the list? It's dishonesty or inauthenticity. "I hate it when someone says one thing and does another," is how it's usually stated. "I can't stand it when people make a promise and then don't come through, or when they put on a false front for people and I know what's really going on inside of them."

Not surprisingly, when I've asked what qualities they find most attractive in others, always near the top of the list are honesty, genuineness, and authenticity. They'll say, "You know, I really like people who back up their words with action." Or, "I appreciate men and women who have the courage to be real, even when it makes them unpopular." Or, "I like it when people are willing to own up to their mistakes."

Time and again, I've found that people are strongly drawn to sincerity. So it follows that one of the most important things you can do to effectively draw in friends and loved ones toward Christ is to simply be real. To avoid acting like more than you are or pretending you're less than what you are. To feel free, through the liberating power of God, to just be you.

Jesus was pleading with His people—then and now—to live in a way that would draw people toward the Father. Think about it; how we conduct our daily lives has implications that reach all the way into eternity.

I once heard a story that illustrates the tremendous temptation to make ourselves appear bigger than we are. It's about a newly promoted colonel who had moved into a recently built makeshift office during the Gulf War. He had just arrived and was getting things organised, when out of the corner of his eye he saw a private coming his way, carrying a tool box.

Wanting to seem important, he quickly spun around and picked up his phone, "Yes, General Schwarzkopf, yes, yes, of course, I think that's an excellent plan," he said. "You've got my support on it. Thanks for checking with me. Let's touch base again soon, Norm. Goodbye." And he briskly hung up and turned around.

"And what can I do for you?" he asked the private. "Ahh, I'm just here to hook up your phone," came the rather sheepish reply.

There's a lot of deception in this world. Pretense abounds. Too many people are trying to be more than they really are. So many pretenders are walking around the corridors of our culture these days that genuine, sincere people wind up creating quite a stir just being themselves.

In order to expand on what I'm talking about, let's touch on four areas related to authenticity that will be attractive to seekers and turn their heads toward heaven.

Just being you

The first is *authentic identity*. I can't tell you how many brand new Christians stop me after our weekend services to say that part of what drew them to Christ was the realisation that there can be great diversity in the makeup of God's family.

I remember one man's saying, "I came to this church expecting the leaders to be pushing everyone into the same mould. And I anticipated hearing that there was a thoroughly defined set of specs for how a Christian should look, act, talk, smell, dress, and think. But guess what? I found exactly the opposite to be true!

"I saw an amazing variety of people: young, old, rich, poor, educated, uneducated, black, white, and everything in between. I heard teaching that affirmed diversity. I heard challenges like, 'Figure out who God made you to be. Discover how He gifted you. Try to discern His special calling on your life, and follow it.' "

He continued by saying, "I was shocked to learn that there was no single mould that everybody had to be crammed into." Then he said something I hope I'll never forget: "I discovered I didn't have to renounce my identity to receive and follow Christ. It blew my mind to learn that God cares deeply about me. He loves the way I'm put together, and He wants to use me in a fashion consistent with the design He gave me."

Do you see the importance of an authentic identity? This man was drawn to Christ through meeting Christians who loved God with all their hearts, souls, minds, and strength, but who did so without abandoning their basic makeup or personality.

One of the greatest mistakes a believer can make is to renounce or repress his God-given uniqueness in a vain attempt to appear more spiritual. That error is deadly on two counts. First, after ten or fifteen years of identity repression you can totally lose your understanding of who you really are. Second, there are some people outside the family of God who will never see Him for who He really is until they watch Him living and working authentically in one of His unique sons or daughters—*one just like you!*

Do you want to be a contagious Christian? Then stop apologising for your God-given design. Quit trying to deny your individuality. Give up on trying to stuff yourself into someone else's mould of what a good Christian should be. That's not the game plan God has in mind for you.

I'm thrilled that a dedicated Christian I know has been recognised as one of the most competitive and intense NFL linebackers in the history of American football. I'm equally excited that another deeply committed Christian friend of mine is a razor-sharp female attorney who fights for the rights of abused and neglected children with the same kind of intensity that Mike Singletary brought to American football.

God designed quite a few people in this world to be intense. And it's great news when seekers learn that they can follow Christ without having to repress or deny their inbred passion for life.

In fact, in the kaleidoscope of God's family, there's room for all gifts and temperaments. God may have given you extraordinary depths of mercy, lots of patience, heights of wisdom, or the ability to enjoy adventure or to thrive on solitude. And, somewhere in your community, there's probably a seeker who's one step away from coming to faith but who needs to come into contact with someone just like you—with *your* personality, *your* temperament, *your* passion, and *your* interests. If that seeker could glimpse how God lives and works through you, it might be enough to propel him across the line of faith.

Psalm 139:14 says we are "fearfully and wonderfully made." As you manifest your uniqueness, you'll become a compelling model that will attract others to your source of personal freedom.

So many pretenders are walking around the corridors of our culture these days that genuine, sincere people wind up creating quite a stir just being themselves.

Being real on the inside

Another powerful magnet that draws people to God is an *authentic emotional life*. Tragically, many Christians have gotten confused about how to express their feelings. Some well-meaning but misguided pastors and leaders have taught that dedicated Christians should never get angry, and that expressing sadness or hurt or grief are signs of low faith or shallow character. Untold numbers of believers have tried to smile and say, "Praise God" in the midst of any and all circumstances, thinking this an indicator of spiritual maturity.

But in their valiant attempts, two negative consequences have emerged. The first is what I call "emotional vertigo". That's when a person outlaws certain feelings for so long that he eventually enters a state of total emotional confusion. In fact, he loses the ability to experience feelings altogether. He doesn't recognise them when they try to break through, or know how to express them to somebody else.

You see, in his desperate attempt to "Christianise" his feelings, he's manipulated them for so long that he's left in a helpless state of emotional apathy and disorientation. It takes a lot of work—and, often, some Christian counselling—to get out of that condition.

The second consequence is that seekers are quickly repelled by emotional inauthenticity. They see red flags all over the place when, for example, a young couple delivers a stillborn baby and then responds to the heart-rending disappointment with dry eyes and a nonstop string of clichéd phrases like, "Thank God anyway."

Seekers just shake their heads and think, "You know, there really should be some serious grieving going on here. Something is dreadfully wrong. Call me a pagan, but losses like this one ought to be mourned, regardless of your religion."

Can I give you an inside scoop? People who are investigating Christianity don't expect perfection from Christians. They're too street-smart for that! What they do hope to find is someone with the courage to confess their blunders and make things right.

Contrast this to the example of Jesus. Remember what He did when His friend Lazarus died? He wept, right out in public. He just broke down and cried openly. And I'm sure that His emotional genuineness further endeared seekers to Him.

Recently I heard a father describe the night he

learned that his eighteen-year-old son had been killed in a car accident. As this dedicated Christian recounted the awful story to me, his eyes filled with tears. For a moment he stopped. Finally he said, "You know, I still feel a hole in my heart almost every hour of every day."

When he finished the story, I felt spiritually drawn to him. And I was attracted to the God who gave him the power to be so vulnerable and real. I thought, this is a liberated man, someone in touch with who he is and with what's going on inside of himself.

Do you know what seekers need to see in you more than dry eyes and pasted-on smiles? They need to see you grapple with fear and sadness and anger and jealousy and loss. They need to hear you talk openly about it. They need to watch you work out your faith without discounting the everyday emotional realities of your life.

So don't hide the struggle that's going on inside. Don't try to sanitise it or Christianise it, because your feelings are important. God built them into you. In fact, He has those feelings, too! And if you'll address them in a healthy and open fashion, your emotional authenticity will point those around you to the God at work within you.

Being forthright about failure

Along similar lines, there is a third area we need to discuss, which is *authentic confession*. This has to do with how dedicated Christians deal with their foul-ups and failures. The problem is that most of us have mistakenly thought we should hide our failures at all costs. We've been told that our moral missteps will drive people away from God, so we'd better not let anyone find out about them.

I'll never forget talking to a business owner who, as a seeker, had employed scores of Christians in his company. He watched them like a hawk. "You know, I was naturally drawn to God by observing Christian workers who were conscientious and kind and thorough and aggressive on the job," he told me. "But I'll tell you what really impressed me. One day a guy who I knew to be a fresh convert asked if he could see me after work. I agreed to meet with him, but later in the day I started to worry that this young religious zealot might be coming to try to convert me, too.

"I was surprised when he came in my office with his head hanging low and said to me, 'Sir, I'll only take a few minutes, but I'm here to ask your forgiveness. Over the years I've worked for you I've done what a lot of other employees do, like borrowing a few company products here and there. And I've taken some extra supplies; I've abused telephone privileges; and I've cheated the time clock now and then.

" 'But I became a Christian a few months ago and it's real—not the smoke and mirror stuff. In gratitude for what Christ has done for me and in obedience to Him, I want to make amends to you and the company for the wrong I've done. So could we figure out a way to do that? If you have to fire me for what I've done, I'll understand. I deserve it. Or, if you want to dock my pay, dock it by whatever figure you think is appropriate. If you want to give me some extra work to do on my own time, that would be okay, too. I just want to make things right with God and between us.' "

Well, they worked things out. And that business owner told me that this conversation made a deeper spiritual impact on him than anything else ever had. It was the single most impressive demonstration of true Christianity he had ever witnessed.

What was it that made this new believer so contagious? Was it a clever new gospel presentation? Was it a well-rehearsed testimony? Obviously not. It was merely a genuine and humble admission of wrongdoing along with a willingness to make it right.

Simply put, authentic confession is a powerful witness to the transforming power of Christ in your life. It stands out in stark contrast to our culture, in which nobody admits to wrongdoing of any kind. This is the age where we rationalise our shortcomings, cover our tracks, and hire successful attorneys to get us off the hook. No one seems to own up to anything anymore.

Seekers have little respect for weak Christians. Deep down they're looking for somebody—anybody—to step up and proclaim the truth and then to live it boldly. And I've just got to ask, why can't that be us?

Taking seriously the directives of the Bible and humbly acknowledging our foul-ups, is the stuff of high-potency Christianity. And it causes the seeker in today's no-fault society to realise that only the influence of the living God would prompt a person to say, "It was my fault and I'm sorry."

So how about it? Do you ever come clean by admitting your wrong-doing? Or are you working overtime to present an image of infallibility to everyone around you, fearing if they knew you were imperfect all would be lost? Don't underestimate the power of a sincere apology. It might be the most compelling manifestation of true Christianity your friends have ever seen.

Perhaps there's something you should confess at work, in your home, or in your neighbourhood. Or there could be an area of your life that you know isn't right, but you're still trying to cover it up in the hope that nobody will find out. Maybe now God's Spirit is prompting you to go to somebody and say, "Because I mean business about my relationship with God and I want to be right before Him and with you, I need to apologise."

Can I give you an inside scoop? People who are investigating Christianity don't expect perfection from Christians. They're too street-smart for that! What they do hope to find is someone with the courage to confess their blunders and make things right. They want to see humility and repentance, and maybe even restitution.

And when they do, it assures them that you're serious about your faith. It gives them confidence that if they give their life to Christ, they're not going to have to live under the tyranny of perfectionism. And, believe me, they'll be relieved and much more open.

Living like we mean it

Let's touch briefly on one more area related to authenticity: *living by genuine conviction*.

Do you remember seeing on television a few years ago the Chinese college student who stood in front of the advancing tank in Tienanmen Square? What went through your mind when you saw that man literally laying down his life in front of that tank? It certainly stirred my spirit and got my blood pumping.

I had similar feelings when I saw the East Germans slamming their pick axes into the Berlin Wall while the soldiers stood there with their rifles pointing at them.

I'm not ashamed to admit that it strikes a cord deep inside of me almost every time I see someone stand up and take a risk or pay a price for something they believe in. Even if I don't agree with the cause they represent, I find myself moved and impressed by the depth of their commitment and their willingness to get off the spectator stands and onto the playing field.

I've learned through the years that seekers are not impressed with spinelessness. I need to emphasise this because many Christians are so afraid that if they state what they really believe, if they come out of the closet, or if they live by biblical priorities, then they'll automatically alienate those outside the faith. But that's almost never the case.

Most of the time, seekers, whether they admit it openly or not, respect and admire Christians who aren't afraid to take a stand. Don't forget, many of them are trying to make up their own minds about what to do with the claims of Christ. So when a believer speaks up for what is right, defends Christianity intelligently, or lives his faith openly and authentically, seekers are forced to deal with the implications for their own lives.

They ask themselves, "What do *I* believe? What would I be willing to take a stand for? Do I have the courage to do what is right like my Christian friend does?" Over time, questions like these often lead to answers found in Christ.

A role model

The Bible describes a Roman centurion who watched the proceedings on the day of Jesus' crucifixion. He stood as a spectator in one of history's greatest dramas. And he looked on as Jesus was thrown to the ground, nailed to the cross, and then displayed for public ridicule. He watched intently as Jesus continued to maintain His claim to be God's Son, the Saviour of the world. He listened as Jesus made provisions for the care of His mother and extended grace to the repentant thief.

Then this battle-hardened soldier shuddered as Jesus courageously cried out, "It is finished...Father, into your hands I commit my spirit."

When Jesus had died, the centurion began to realise

the cost of it all, the depth of Jesus' commitment to His mission, and His willingness to give up His very life. This man was tortured by what had been played out in front of him. His mind was filled with chaos. And eventually his heart came to the point of admitting what his head knew to be true. He finally cried out from the depth of his being, "Surely this man was the Son of God!"

Nothing short of Jesus' willingness to lay down His life would have brought that cynical Roman soldier to his knees. It was Jesus' genuine and courageous devotion to His mission that wrung that declaration out of the centurion.

The challenge

Let me say it once more: Seekers have little respect for weak Christians. Deep down they're looking for somebody—anybody—to step up and proclaim the truth and then to live it boldly. And I've just got to ask, *why can't that be us*? Why can't we live authentically and boldly on our job sites, in our neighbourhoods, at our schools, and in our world? What are we so afraid of? What's holding us back? We have the Holy Spirit, we have the Word of God, and we have the church.

We want to be contagious Christians, don't we? Then let's be real with people. Let's manifest an authentic identity and not be more or less than God made us to be. Let's be emotionally authentic and grapple with whatever life throws at us. Let's humbly admit errors when we make them.

And let's boldly stand up for what we believe. Let's declare it and live it out, without apology, in order to provoke the kind of decision the centurion made.

That's the power, attractiveness, and potential of an authentic Christian life.

CHAPTER FIVE

The Pull of Compassion

"So tell me, what are you doing to help poor people in your neighbourhood? Do you have any programmes to feed the hungry or to clothe the needy or to shelter the homeless?"

As I've travelled to various parts of the world to talk about what Willow Creek Community Church is doing to reach irreligious people, these kinds of questions inevitably come up. I'm glad that they keep getting asked.

That's because I find it encouraging that so many people in so many locations, from both Christian and non-Christian perspectives, understand that caring for the tangible needs of human beings is part-and-parcel of genuine Christianity. They seem to have an innate awareness of James 1:27: "Religion that God our Father accepts as pure and faultless is this: to look after orphans and widows in their distress. . . ."

The critical nature of compassion is echoed throughout the Bible. In the Old Testament, God says, "I command you to be openhanded toward your brothers and toward the poor and needy in your land" (Deuteronomy 15:11). In the New Testament, Jesus brought it closer to home: "I tell you the truth, whatever you did for one of the least of these brothers of mine, you did for me" (Matthew 25:40). And after describing the commissioning of Barnabas and himself by the church in

Jerusalem, Paul recounts in Galatians 2:10, "All they asked was that we should continue to remember the poor, the very thing I was eager to do."

When action-oriented compassion is absent, it's a tell-tale sign that something's spiritually amiss. Whether the problem is with the organisation or the individual, uncaring Christianity does not attract inquirers into its fold. But a clear and consistent demonstration of Christ-like love is a powerful magnet that pulls people toward Him.

A road-side illustration

Jesus illustrated the importance of compassion in one of His most famous stories, found in Luke 10. It's about a Jewish man who was walking from Jerusalem toward the city of Jericho. He got part of the way there when some thugs jumped out from behind the rocks. They robbed him, stripped him, beat him up, and left him half-conscious in the ditch on the side of the road.

A short time later a priest came walking along. The wounded traveller saw him coming and thought his luck was finally turning, but the priest walked over to the far side of the road without even slowing down. A little while later another religious man, a Levite, came along. To the injured man's dismay, he too passed by quickly.

Then, Jesus told His listeners, a man from Samaria came down the road. Even though there was a lot of ethnic strife between Samaritans and Jews, this Samaritan felt compassion for the robbery victim and stopped to see how he could help. After assessing the situation, he knelt down over him, poured oil and wine on his wounds, and bandaged him up.

Then he lifted the Jewish man onto his donkey and took him to an inn, where he made sure the man had a clean, warm bed. He even gave the innkeeper some money. "I'll cover the tab as long as it takes for this man to get well," he told him. "You take care of him and I'll come by later to pay any additional expenses."

I've often wondered what went through the mind of this robbed and beaten Jewish man when he woke up the next day in a comfortable bed, all bandaged up, and his room and board paid for by someone he didn't even know. "Who did this?" I'll bet he asked. "Why didn't he turn away like everybody else?"

Aren't those the kind of questions that are often asked by people on the receiving end of compassion? They want to look behind the generous act itself to get a glimpse of the underlying motivation. "Why would *anyone* do something like this for me," they ask in bewilderment.

The call to compassion

One of the primary reasons God calls His followers to be extraordinarily caring people is because acts of mercy open up people's hearts like nothing else can. Put another way, there's tremendous pulling power in the expression of even a single act of kindness. And God wants that power to draw people toward the reality of His Son.

Jesus spelled this out in John 13:34–35: "A new commandment I give you: Love one another. As I have loved you, so you must love one another. All men will know that you are my disciples if you love one another." How simple, yet how powerful!

As we express compassion to each other, people will recognise it as an earmark of authentic Christianity. It helps them better understand what God is like, who His children are, and why they should personally trust Him too.

How often lately have you felt compassion for people

in need? Have you followed up those feelings and actually helped someone by serving them, encouraging them, visiting them, or by expressing love in some other tangible way?

To help you quantify your response, I'd like to challenge you to write down a number that represents your present level of compassion toward others. We'll call it your personal compassion quotient. Pick a number from zero to ten, with zero meaning you're heart is completely cold, and ten suggesting you're a Mother Teresa clone.

Be sure to indicate what your quotient is *now*, not what it was a few years ago or what you'd like it to be in the future. And, to spice things up a little, I'm going to ban the number five! That way, you've got to lean your score in one direction or the other. Now, write down your number on a piece of paper or in the column of this page. Got it?

When action-oriented compassion is absent, it's a tell-tale sign that something's spiritually amiss. Whether the problem is with the organisation or the individual, uncaring Christianity does not attract inquirers into its fold.

A personal lesson

Several years ago while I was on a study break in Michigan, I was reflecting on Jesus' parable of the Good Samaritan. I remember sitting alone in a booth at a little diner, choking back tears as I read and reread those verses. I was overwhelmed by the realisation that my personal compassion quotient had become *dangerously* low.

Along with that disheartening admission came the reminders of 1 Corinthians 13:1–3:

> If I speak in the tongues of men and of angels, but have not love, I am only a resounding gong or a clanging cymbal. If I have the gift of prophecy and can fathom all mysteries and all knowledge, and if I have a faith that can move mountains, but have not love, I am nothing. If I give all I possess to the poor and surrender my body to the flames, but have not love, I gain nothing.

These verses, which are so often read like some sort of flowery poetry, hit me right between the eyes. I had to own up to the fact that I was failing in the very area to which God attached the greatest significance: *love*. It was difficult to admit to myself that this divine commodity, which I had experienced so abundantly from God and people, and that I had often taught others about, was so lacking in my own life.

But in His characteristically gentle yet firm way, God led me through the shame, guilt, and embarrassment that came with that realisation. And as a result of that soul-stretching experience, I learned some things that helped me make some radical changes in the way I live. For the rest of the chapter I'll detail some of what I learned.

I'm glad to say that since then, there's been a gradual improvement in my personal compassion quotient. It certainly has its ups and downs, and I have a long way to go. My accountability group helps by keeping an eye on me to make sure I'm headed in the right direction. Compassion is not an easy area for me, but I'm thankful to report that overall my heart's expanding rather than contracting.

I had to own up to the fact that I was failing in the very area to which God attached the greatest significance: love. It was difficult to admit to myself that this divine commodity, which I had experienced so abundantly from God and people, and that I had often taught others about, was so lacking in my own life.

As I've seized opportunities to put love and concern for people into concrete action, I've seen the hearts of seekers start to melt and become soft toward God, the source of all compassion. I've even had the thrill of seeing some of them come all the way to the point of committing their lives to Christ! When *that* happens, it makes me all the more hungry to see ever-increasing amounts of this sort of action in my life.

I'll bet you'd like to see more of that kind of thing happen around you, too. If so, then let's look at what it'll take to keep your personal compassion quotient high.

Some compassion busters

Will you let me play the role of a heart doctor and do a little diagnostic investigating? This exploratory work will especially apply to you if your current compassion quotient score was six or less. If it was, you may feel some of the same emotions I experienced that day in Michigan several years ago. Don't let that discourage you; let it drive you toward action. If your score was higher than that, perhaps you'll find some ideas to help you raise it up to the next notch.

Let's examine a few factors that may be sabotaging your score. Then we'll prescribe some ideas for making appropriate changes.

Where you live

The first potential problem is that you may have come from, or may still be living in, a defeating home or work environment. It's a simple but often overlooked fact that compassion breeds compassion. Love produces love. Merciful environs foster merciful attitudes.

So some of us enjoy relatively high compassion quotients simply because we were raised in loving homes. Our childhood memories are filled with laughter and love and security and acceptance. Others among us have the distinct advantage of working in a healthy vocational setting that's motivating and uplifting, and that tends to buoy our quotient.

If I'm describing you, let me encourage you to bow your head right now and breathe a fervent prayer of thanksgiving to God, because you are a blessed man or woman. Your compassion quotient, by virtue of your positive upbringing or encouraging work situation alone, might be in the seven to nine range. Don't take that for granted, because there are so many others who are trying to recuperate from an upbringing that started them out in deficit range.

Many people learned the hard way, very early in life, that contempt breeds contempt. Anger produces more anger. Hatred feeds hatred. And abuse results in nonstop nightmares. If that's you, it's hard to know how to react to the "Norman Rockwell" family backgrounds that some of us had. On the one hand, you want to rejoice and say, "I'm so glad for you." On the other, you feel like crying out: "Why couldn't my home have been like that? All I ever knew was fear, or hurt, or betrayal, or heartbreak. How am I supposed to spread mercy, when I can barely even relate to that emotion?"

Countless numbers of people have said to me, "I never once felt mercy or love from either of my parents. I didn't have any relatives or important people in my life who treasured me. I've never even had a friend who I knew loved me deeply." No wonder they have difficulty knowing how to manifest compassion toward others!

Add to that a defeating work situation of the kind Michael Maccoby observed and described in his book, *The Gamesman*. "The most loving [people] were not the ones who moved up the ladder rapidly," he said about the current American workplace. "Corporate work stimulates and rewards qualities of the head and not the heart."

Or as a businessman confided to me recently, "Something very sick has happened in our company culture in the past five years. For me to keep my job these days, I have to check my heart at the door." Then he looked down and said, "The problem is, I often forget to retrieve it on my way home."

Can you relate to what he's saying? Maybe you're in an extremely competitive business where it's pretty safe to assume that the other players aren't wringing their hands about having low scores on the kindness scale. They're the type who'll sink to any depth to get a deal done. And there you are, trying your best to honour God and contagiously point others to Christ by showing love to others.

If that's you, I'll bet you sometimes feel a sinister sense of schizophrenia, don't you? You want to be a compassionate person, but you can't figure out how to survive at work without leaving your heart at the front door. So you feel depressed, and sometimes hypocritical, for living one way in church on Sunday and then operating another way when you're at work on Monday.

It's easy to see how some people end up with a low compassion rating. Their home or work environment has them defeated before they even get to the starting blocks.

Maybe you need to address the lingering effects of a destructive upbringing by talking it through with a wise friend or Christian counsellor. If you're still living in that situation, you'll need to take some courageous steps to either change the environment or move into a more healthy one.

Or perhaps it's your work setting that's beating you down. Don't you get tired of letting the people at the job site sway you in the wrong direction? Are you willing to let God lead and empower you to take some positive action steps, whether they be minor adjustments or something more radical—possibly even changing jobs?

Life is too short and the world too compassion-starved for you to keep subsisting in situations that drag you down and curtail your potential to help advance the Kingdom. There's just too much at stake. God really is able and willing to help you make environment-improving changes.

How you live

Another reason some of us end up with low compassion quotients is that we try to maintain an unhealthy pace of life.

Think back to the parable of the Good Samaritan. I believe that the priest and the Levite were, at heart, kind and compassionate people. Most people in professional religious careers are; or at least they start out that way. But something often happens to them, and the same thing can affect the rest of us as well. We plunge into our careers, then we start raising our families, we deal with ever-increasing financial demands—and life keeps getting faster and faster and faster.

Life is too short and the world too compassion-starved for you to keep subsisting in situations that drag you down and curtail your potential to help advance the Kingdom. There's just too much at stake.

It's not just in our minds. Lou Harris conducted a poll comparing what happened in the American work place in 1988 with fifteen years earlier. The average work week jumped from 41 to 47 hours. For those in management, it soared to the range of 52-59 hours per week. During that same period, actual leisure time shrunk thirty-seven per cent. Add to this the pressure of two-career families or the incredible weight of running a single-parent household, and the result is that many people are living in what I refer to as "crisis mode".

Crisis mode is where your speed just keeps accelerating out of control. When you're in it, you start finding yourself using all your spare moments to figure out how you're going to keep all the balls in the air and all the plates spinning.

Doesn't it almost go without saying that people consistently living in crisis mode are generally not big distributors of compassion? They're just trying to survive their own weekly drill. They feel they can't expend precious emotional energy to dole out warmth and kindness to people who are down on their luck. It's every man for himself!

Knowing the demands and pressures associated with

church work, I can almost hear the priest and the Levite whispering to themselves as they passed by the wounded traveller: "You think *you've* got problems? *I've* got six more meetings before sundown!"

Or, as a stressed-out executive told me recently, "I have learned that to make it in my career, I have to put everything outside of work on indefinite hold, including this notion of compassion." Leaders aren't the only ones living with their RPM's past redline. Parents of young children, working mums, and over-committed church members sometimes look at their haggard faces in the mirror and ask themselves, "How long am I going to live like this? Am I honouring God by living so insanely?"

An unhealthy pace of life may be destructive in a dozen different ways, but this one is for sure: It will suppress your compassion quotient. You don't have the time or the emotional energy to tune in to people who are in need. Somewhere deep down you want to, but you feel like you just can't afford to do anything about it.

Leaders aren't the only ones living with their RPM's past redline. Parents of young children, working mums, and over-committed church members sometimes look at their haggard faces in the mirror and ask themselves, "How long am I going to live like this? Am I honouring God by living so insanely?"

Again, I'm speaking from experience. In the ebb and flow of my life, I can always tell I've let my schedule get out of control when I find myself routinely passing up chances to express compassion because I simply lack the energy or time. But when I consciously take steps to bring down the pace of my life, I find time and again that both my desire and my opportunities to show love and mercy to others naturally increase.

Once Lynne and I were speaking away from home, and we were having breakfast in a little restaurant. I noticed that the waitress seemed upset, and it looked like she was fighting back tears. After watching her for a while, I started to feel concern for her welling up inside of me. So I waited for an opportune moment, and then I quietly walked up and asked if I could help her in some way.

"No, but thanks. Thank you so much," she said. "You see, my former husband is coming today to get my fifteen-year-old daughter. I'm not going to get to see her again for six months, and it's hard. It's really hard."

I touched her shoulder, and said, "I'm sorry. I know I can't do anything to change the situation, but I really feel sad for you. My wife and I are over at that table if you want to talk or pray, or if we can help in any way, but I just wanted you to know we care, and I wish we could help in some way."

Then I sat back down. Soon after that, things got busy in the restaurant, so we weren't able to talk anymore. But when we left she gave me an appreciative glance.

You know, at that moment I felt empathy that I hadn't felt for a long, long time. Later that day I just basked in the realisation that my slower pace of life was finally enabling me to feel compassion on a more regular basis. I'm starting to live again with an emotional reserve that can be tapped any time an opportunity presents itself. And for you, maybe just getting out of crisis mode will bump your compassion quotient up two or three notches. But for that to happen, soooner or later you're going to have to take some radical action to slow things down.

How you give

A third possible explanation for low compassion quotients affects fewer people, but if you're one of them, it's an important area to talk about. It's the problem that results from excessive care-giving.

Believe it or not, it's possible to overdose on expressing compassion. I know some people in our church who early in their Christian lives got so involved that they sort of unzipped their chests and offered their hearts to every needy person who came their way. They were so overwhelmed by God's grace that they wanted to be conduits of His love to every troubled person they could find. And so they gave and gave; in fact, they gave so excessively they were ready to give out.

Then one day they found themselves feeling a tinge of resentment toward someone they were caring for. But they didn't let it slow them down, at least not at first. Instead, they ignored the warning signal and gave still more, although their hearts weren't in it as much as before.

Then the roof caved in. At a certain point these people said, "This is crazy! I'm caring for everyone else, but who's caring for me? I feel so empty, angry, and confused. I give and give and give, but nobody gives back." And, as you would predict, the care-giving pendulum swings all the way back over to the "Who gives a toss about others" side, and the "It's my turn now" side. Unfortunately, in many cases it stays over there for many years.

Maybe you've become cold-hearted, not because you're that way naturally, but because in the past you let your care-giving get out of control. You got burned so badly that your pendulum is stuck on the other side. Now when you hear appeals to help needy people, you sort of tremble inside and automatically react by telling yourself, "I just can't do it! Remember what happened before? It almost ruined my life!"

Unfortunately, many people never learned that caring for others has to be meticulously balanced with caring for yourself. This is how to prevent burn-out in the process of giving compassion, and it's a pattern that Jesus often demonstrated. He gave out enormous amounts of care, but then on a regular basis He said, in effect, "Enough is enough. Now I'm going to the mountain to pray and be alone, where I can rest and recuperate."

There's a time for giving to others and, as Ecclesiastes 3:1–8 indicates, a time for the opposite: taking care of yourself. That means laying back, putting your feet up, laughing, enjoying life, and through God's natural timing, letting your compassion reserves refill.

What you've received

Let me offer one final explanation for why some of us have low compassion scores. As we mentioned earlier, love breeds love and compassion produces compassion. So it stands to reason that people who regularly enjoy fresh touches of love from the hand of God are then going to turn around and extend a similar kind of grace and kindness to other people. We're conduits of God's love, not reservoirs.

Mother Teresa put it well: "The wire is you and me; the current is God," she said. "We have the power to let the current pass through us, use us, and produce the light of the world—Jesus."

Occasionally, people like you and me receive touches of grace and compassion from God, but we forget that Ephesians 5:1 says to "be imitators of God, therefore, as dearly loved children." So we fail to cooperate with His conduit plan. We receive good gifts from Him in the form of salvation, guidance, a new relationship, forgiveness, answered prayer, and sometimes a miraculous provision for something in our lives. But we just absorb it all without passing it on to others, and as a result our compassion quotient drops.

We're like the penniless debtor described by Jesus in Matthew 18. This man had piled up enormous indebtedness, and then payback day came. His creditor said, "Sorry, but a deal is a deal. If you can't pay your debts, I'll sell you and your pretty wife and all your children into slavery where you can spend the rest of your lives working it off."

The man panicked. He knew he couldn't repay the debt if he worked an entire lifetime. So he swallowed his pride and fell on his face. "Master, have mercy on me," he implored. "If there's an ounce of kindness in you, be gracious to me. Please, I beg you."

And, lo and behold, the powerful creditor was moved with compassion and forgave the entire debt. He tore up the bank note, torched the loan papers, and declared, "All right, you're free." Talk about compassion! Can you imagine how overwhelmed that man must have felt? Free! The debt had been cancelled.

But did that man let compassion produce compassion in his life? Did he spread kindness to everyone in his path? No!

Just think what would happen in your home, your family, your workplace, or your school if your quotient went up three or four positions! How many more lives would be touched?

The Bible says he turned around and grabbed the

lapels of a guy who owed him just a few pounds. "Pay up, buddy," he snarled, "or I'll press charges to the fullest extent of the law!" To this his debtor exclaimed, "I'll need a little bit of time. I need some grace. Would you please be compassionate toward me?" But the man said, "No way. Don't you know a deal is a deal?" And he had him arrested and thrown into jail.

You know the conclusion. The original creditor finds out about this travesty, calls the scoundrel in, and says to him, "You pleaded for mercy from me and I gave it to you in abundance. I overwhelmed you with compassion. And now you turn the screws on a poor guy who owes you a mere five pounds? Bad move, pal. Bad move. Now you're going to pay—you and your family for the rest of your lives."

You see, Jesus was using this story to reinforce the fact that mercy ought to produce mercy. Grace should produce grace. And as Christians, we are by definition recipients of *amazing* grace.

Like the penniless debtor, we piled up enormous debts of sin that none of us could pay off even in a thousand lifetimes. Our only hope was kindness from God. And, wonder of wonders, He extended His compassion on Good Friday, when Christ paid the debt for our sins. The day you received His gift, He torched the list of offenses you had accumulated.

The memory of when I received His gift is as clear to me as the day it happened. I wanted to climb the highest mountain and shout, "I'm free! I'm free! My sin has been forgiven! My debt has been cancelled! God is a compassionate God!" I also remember how intensely I wanted to extend His compassion to others. Five-pound debts here and there didn't mean a thing to me anymore because I had an overflow of the grace of God to pour into as many lives as possible.

Perhaps you've gone a long time without a fresh,

personal experience of God's compassion. Perhaps you, like Job, have wondered if God has removed His presence and love from you. In Job 23:8–9, this man who suffered so much laments: "But if I go to the east, he is not there; if I go to the west, I do not find him. When he is at work in the north, I do not see him; when he turns to the south, I catch no glimpse of him."

Philip Yancey, in his book *Disappointment with God*, describes many people who have sensed a lack of God's presence in their lives. If you feel like a dead current, desperate for a jolt of God's love and compassion, you're certainly not alone.

Do you remember days in your life when you received God's grace? In addition to your conversion experience, can you recall any miraculous provisions? New relationships that have brought joy or encouragement? Guidance through murky waters? Strength through tough times? Surprises of grace? When you look back, I think you'll see that God has dealt mercifully with you, not just at the point of salvation, but every day since then. And even if you haven't noticed it lately, God's kindness and compassion will always be there for you, even through the hard eras of your life.

But some of us become accustomed to grace. We take God's kindness for granted. We get used to receiving His compassion and we wind up expecting it, absorbing it, and failing to pass it on to others. Then we find ourselves ignoring needy people or, worse yet, demanding five-pound repayments from people instead of being conduits of God's compassion and love. We need to be reminded of God's care and kindness toward us, as well as His plan to love and attract others through us.

Raising your quotient

Are you satisfied with your compassion quotient as it stands today? Have you recognised any problem areas where it's being driven down? Do you see some places that need work in order to raise your quotient a notch or two? Just think what would happen in your home, your family, your work-place, or your school if your quotient went up three or four positions! How many more lives would be touched? Imagine how many people would say, "There really *might* be a God, because look at how much love there is flowing from that person. Who else could create that sort of kindness inside a human being?"

Is an unhealthy home or work environment tripping you up? Ask God to guide and empower you to either stand up to the opposition or to move away from it. Remember that 1 Corinthians 10:13 promises an escape hatch of one kind or another. Claim that promise and follow God's lead.

Has your pace of life been dragging down your score? Only you can figure out what it'll take to throttle back and spend less time in crisis mode. And when you do, you'll find your compassion quotient naturally rebounding.

Or maybe you've slipped into excessive care-giving. You can relate to the feelings of bitterness we talked about earlier. You've given out more than you've taken in, and now you've given out! It's time to follow the pattern of Jesus by beginning to develop a more healthy mix of rest, relaxation, recreation, and restorative relationships.

Finally, are you frustrated from trying to communicate something to others that you're not experiencing yourself? Do you need to get some fresh touches of God's love so you'll have something to pass on to others?

Each person is different. One may need to get away to the woods to pray and to worship God. Someone else may require fellowship and interaction with other committed Christians who will encourage her and usher her into intimacy with God. For some, it's a matter of eliminating sinful attitudes or behaviours. For others, there's a need to feed their minds on the Scriptures, to remind themselves of who God is and how He loves them. Do whatever it takes for *you* to sense His presence and feel His compassion.

But when you do, remember not to bottle it up. His plan is for you to receive His mercy and then let it produce a merciful spirit in you so that you can pass it on to other people. Let His love and grace affect others through you!

It'll be worth whatever it takes for us to raise our compassion quotient. As our lives become more and more Christ-like, we become increasingly contagious to others.

CHAPTER SIX

The Strength of Sacrifice

"He gave his life for me."

I was emotionally moved as I sat in my study and watched this young soldier on a television newscast. He seemed almost unaware of the TV reporter who was intruding into his private moment of contemplation and relived memories.

They were at the Vietnam Veteran's Memorial in Washington, D.C. The soldier was by the black granite wall, which is etched with the names of all the Americans who lost their lives in the Vietnam War.

He just stood there, tearfully staring at the wall and tracing his finger over the letters of another soldier's name engraved there. He never even looked at the reporter or the camera, but you could feel his pain. "He gave his life for me," was all he whispered as he kept moving his finger across his friend's name.

As I sat there feeling a small dose of what this soldier must have been experiencing, it struck me that he would be affected for the rest of his life because someone had been willing to sacrifice *everything* for him.

Sacrifices move people. They melt people. They stop people in their tracks and make them ask, "Why? Why would *you* go out of your way for *me*? What would motivate you to put my interests before your own?"

Has someone ever melted your heart by sacrifice done

on your behalf? Has anyone put your concerns in front of their own in a way that really cost them something? If so, I'll bet it stays fresh in your memory. Sacrificial acts are rarely forgotten.

Many years ago I took a trip through Central and South America. I remember visiting a remote tribe in Central America that was only accessible by river. As a friend and I finished our business in that dirty and impoverished Indian village, we were invited to dinner by one of the local families.

While sitting on mats on the dirt floor of their small, candle-lit hut, we watched as our hosts graciously emptied their wooden shelf of its few supplies in order to provide a meal for us. As they were doing this, I happened to notice anxious looks on their children's faces. Then it dawned on me: They were concerned that our dinner was going to deplete their reserves and cause them to go hungry the next day.

That thought haunted me throughout the meal. So after we had eaten, I pulled out some money and tried to reimburse them for the food, but they would have no part of it. You see, they *wanted* to make that sacrifice in order to express their love and hospitality to us. And more than two decades later, I still haven't forgotten that episode.

Sacrifices impact people for a lifetime. And in a day when narcissistically "looking out for number one" has been elevated to an art form, almost *any* kind of sacrifice will cause a stir.

Small investments with big dividends

Some time ago Mark was buying a few things at a grocery store, and he decided to pick up some flowers for his wife, Heidi. While waiting to pay, he struck up a conversation with an elderly woman who was waiting in line in front of him.

"I remember when my husband used to bring me flowers," she said pensively and with some emotion in her voice. "But he died many years ago."

It was obvious to Mark how much she still missed her husband, even after all these years. He tried to say some things that would cheer and encourage her until she had made her purchases and said goodbye.

She left the store while his things were being rung up. Then, suddenly, an idea hit him: *Go and give her your wife's flowers!* So he hurriedly paid for the things he was buying, ran outside, and found the woman walking across the car park. He held out the bouquet to her, "Your husband isn't available to do this, so I'd like to give you these," he said, feeling a mixture of excitement and embarrassment.

Well, as you might imagine, this small sacrifice made a deep impression. In fact, she insisted that he come to her home for tea, and they had a wonderful time getting to know each other.

Since that time Mark and Heidi have lived in five different places. But that woman recently took the effort to find out where they now live, and sent them a package that included gifts for their kids and a letter telling how even now—*ten years later*—she talks to her friends about Mark's act of kindness and how it encouraged her.

Do you see how even the smallest acts of sacrifice are big deals these days? We live in such a self-absorbed world that any selfless activity on behalf of others stands out in sharp contrast.

The Bible says that those of us who follow Christ should live infectious Christian lives. We should live in a way that makes our faith irresistible to those outside the family of God. As Philippians 2:15 says, our lives should "shine like stars in the universe." Or, recalling the illustration of salt, we should have high savour and potency so we can impact those around us.

We've already seen the attractiveness of authenticity and felt the pull of compassion. But as we finish out our section on "The Prerequisite of High Potency", I've got to tell you that we've saved the strongest and most contagious characteristic for last—sacrifice.

Sacrifices move people. They melt people. They stop people in their tracks and make them ask, "Why? Why would you go out of your way for me?"

Think about it. Sometimes authenticity fails to grab people's attention; compassion is occasionally written off as the opiate of do-gooders who may have some ulterior motive. But *sacrifice*, motivated by genuine love and concern, is extremely difficult to discount. It just screams for a response of some kind, which is probably a large part of why Jesus lived such a sacrificial life and then called us to follow in His steps.

Three sacrificial gifts

Though there are many ways we can show love by sacrificing for others, I'm going to focus on three specific areas that I think have the highest impact on people in our culture. When we give of ourselves in these ways, it will almost assuredly gain attention and, over time, pique curiosity. We touched on some of these briefly in chapter two when we looked at the costs of contagious Christianity, seen from our own vantage point. Now we're going to explore their affect on other people.

Maximising your moments

You may have already guessed this first one, and its impact is huge. It's the sacrifice of *time*. Time, as they say, is money, and it's becoming about as rare of a commodity. Work weeks are longer, leisure breaks are shorter, and the pace of life is faster. *USA Today* recently poked fun at the madness of most of our schedules, calculating that if we did all we're supposed to do to live what the experts say is a balanced, well-rounded life, it would require forty-two hours a day to get it all done! It's tough enough to keep all the do-or-die activities afloat without trying to maintain a daily regimen of exercising, flossing, keeping up on world events, enjoying a hobby, and nourishing deep, meaningful friendships with lots of people. It's not *difficult* to do it all; it's *impossible*.

Well, in the midst of a world like that, you make a huge statement to others when you joyfully offer them the gift of time. It's no insignificant gesture.

And it wasn't in Jesus' day, either. Do you remember what Jesus did when He passed through the city of Jericho on a teaching journey in Luke 19? There was a huge crowd of people following Him at this stage of His ministry—something like a parade without the floats!

Suddenly Jesus surprised everyone when He stopped the procession and asked a man named Zacchaeus if he could spare a few hours to have a leisurely dinner together to discuss spiritual issues. Zacchaeus must have gasped in disbelief. But he consented to the meal, and before the stroke of midnight he was a different man! He had experienced a spiritual birth that transformed him from the inside out.

The key to his conversion was that Jesus gave him time. He stopped the parade and focused His attention on this one person. And, as a result, Zacchaeus's future was forever altered.

Zacchaeus was like a lot of people you know. He was interested in the spiritual dimension of his life. He was open enough to look for a strategic place along the parade route to catch a glimpse of Christ. But to help him past the curiosity stage, *somebody* had to sacrifice the time to set up the dinner and turn the conversation in the direction of spiritual matters. Jesus took the time, and that made the difference.

Almost all of us rub shoulders every day with people who are seeking. They're looking for someone who will take the time and effort required to help them come to some solid conclusions about spiritual truth. You can see it in their eyes, can't you? Just look beneath the veneer, and you'll detect a longing for something deeper, something real and true and enduring.

Most of us grossly underestimate the effect we could have on people's eternities if we would take the time to schedule a breakfast or lunch with lost people in our sphere of influence. If we'd just make an appointment, and then take a risk in the conversation by clearly expressing the essence of what it means to know Christ personally, heaven only knows what might happen.

Sometimes authenticity fails to grab people's attention; compassion is occasionally written off as the opiate of do-gooders who may have some ulterior motive. But sacrifice, motivated by genuine love and concern, is extremely difficult to discount.

Recently I heard the testimony of a man named John, who serves in our church's music ministry and plays saxophone in our band. He said that throughout his life there was a voice inside of him crying out, "I wish I knew the way to God. Music isn't doing it for me. Religious effort isn't getting me there. I don't know which way to turn."

But then someone from our band befriended John and invested time in him, even arranging for the two of them to listen to some tapes on basic Christianity so that John could understand the difference between religion and what it means to truly have a relationship with Christ.

Finally, John got it! He grasped the gospel and acted on it by receiving the forgiveness and leadership of Christ. And now he serves our church week in and week out by arranging and performing music that will attract others like himself who need to hear the message, too.

What strikes me is that the most costly sacrifice John's friend gave was time. To do so, he had to take time away from something else—something probably worthwhile and important—to give that gift to John.

I'm sure part of what drew John to Christ was the impact of all the hours this friend was devoting to him. He must have found himself wondering, "Why is this guy willing to spend so much time with me? He must really believe in what he's telling me, and he must genuinely care about my understanding it, because I can't believe the sacrifices he's making for me."

The sacrifice of time combined with clear communication of truth resulted in another sinner finding the Saviour.

We've seen this happen repeatedly in our Seeker Small Group ministry at Willow Creek. Designed for people who are actively checking out Christianity, these groups include a trained leader and at least two apprentices, along with a handful of spiritual seekers. They provide an exciting environment for honest investigation and discussion of biblical truths.

But what's been fascinating is that on a number of occasions the seeking individual has been ready and willing to commit his or her life to Christ after the first or second meeting—sometimes even during an initial interview! That was the case with Barry, who signed up to be in a group with Garry Poole, our staff member who heads up this ministry.

Before the group had even started, Barry called to say that his questions about Christianity were too pressing to wait for the members to get together. So the two of them met and spent an afternoon talking about spiritual issues. Later that night, Barry called Garry to report that he had prayed to ask Jesus Christ to forgive and lead him. All it took was a bit of time invested by a leader who was evangelistically sensitive enough to see the opportunity and run with it.

Have you given anybody the gift of time lately? When was the last time you hit the pause button on your overburdened schedule and just gave away an hour or two to a spiritual seeker?

In an age when most people are intoxicated with the desire for money and material goods, all you have to do to raise a seeker's eyebrows is to put their material needs before yours. These days that might even make the headlines!

Let's be honest: It takes courage and tenacity to clamp down on old habits of overwork and frenetic activity. Downshifting your pace of life is never easy, but it's often necessary. That's why our discussion in the last chapter about lowering our RPMs was so important. We need to have the emotional reserves to express compassion to others. And a side benefit to slowing down your life is having the additional hours available here and there to invest in a modern-day Zacchaeus like John or Barry.

I was reminded of the importance of time during a recent out-of-town speaking engagement. A woman waited in line to talk to me after the programme. When she finally got up to me, this woman, who I didn't know, put her hands on my shoulders and said, "Bill, I've been waiting for years to tell you this. A long time ago I started going to your church, but I was confused spiritually. After I'd been attending for a while, I decided to try to catch you after a service. You had talked to a number of people that day, and you were getting ready to leave when I stopped you and asked if you could explain what it means to become a Christian.

"You gave me the gift of time," she said. "You stayed there a long time and explained to me how I could receive Christ. And later that day I prayed to do just that! I've walked with Christ ever since that day. He's changed my life, and He's changing my family's life, too. I just wanted to say thank you for taking some time to help me."

I drove home that night and thought, "What a payoff! Someone with a transformed life today and heaven tomorrow—because I gave the gift of time." And I prayed that I would never hold back that gift where there was an opportunity like that to be used by God to make an impact.

Reinvesting your resources

A second kind of sacrifice that turns the heads of people searching for spiritual reality is the giving up of resources. "Money isn't everything," we've heard it said, "but it sure beats whatever's in second place!" In an age when most people are intoxicated with the desire for money and material goods, all you have to do to raise a seeker's eyebrows is to put their material needs before yours. These days that might even make the headlines!

A single mum stopped me after I had spoken at one of our weekend services. She was sobbing so hard that I had to steady her for a moment. After she regained her composure, she told me the encouraging story of how she came to faith.

"For years I drove by this campus on Algonquin Road," she said. "Every time I turned and looked at your church, I scoffed at the idea of there being a God, a Son of God named Jesus, a heaven, or a hell. I was happily married, financially secure, and had three wonderful children. I couldn't understand why people were naive enough to get sucked into religion.

"Then the roof caved in on my life. My husband and I experienced devastating financial setbacks. Marital unrest developed, and it progressed from shouting sessions to shoving matches, and I eventually lost. I lost my marriage. I lost our money. I lost everything."

She went on, "When I first came to this church several months ago, I was probably the neediest person in the northwest suburbs of Chicago. I don't think you can imagine the impact the people of this church had on me! These Christians who were perfect strangers—and who I used to deride as I drove by—they loved me, they cared for me, and they took me in. They didn't just say 'Be warm and be fed and go on your way'; they rolled up their sleeves and helped me out in tangible ways.

"The people in the church's food pantry provided groceries for my children and me for a long time. They *fed* my family. Those serving in the cars ministry provided us with reliable transporation, because my husband had taken off with our car. The benevolence team gave me a financial grant to help us get through the roughest period. The budget counselling ministry advised me on how to live within my restricted fiscal limits. The careers ministry helped me learn how to find a job. The Rainbows ministry encouraged my kids, who were living with heartbreak. And some counsellors in the church helped me deal with my own grief and frustration."

Are you a sprinter or a marathon runner? Might you have some family members who are saying, "I'm going to just sit back and watch you"? Why not decide right now that with God's help you're going to wear down every cynic, scoffer, and doubter in your life.

Then she started to break down again. Finally, she blurted out through her tears: "And because of the provisions and assistance of the people of this church, I've also discovered the love of Christ! I just wish I knew how to thank everybody!"

Well, by that time she wasn't the only one with tears in her eyes. Her story touched me deeply. Our encounter gave me a new appreciation for the impact that can come from sharing resources with others.

If you've ever stared at an eviction notice or repossession papers, if you've ever had your heart pound when the phone rings because you're afraid it's another creditor, if you've ever lacked the basics necessary to function in the world and you knew that "D-Day" was approaching without any apparent way out, then you know how overwhelmed and appreciative people feel when a generous Christian joyfully and eagerly reaches into his resource barrel and helps meet those needs. The person on the receiving end of a transaction like that lays awake at night staring at the ceiling, trying to figure out what would make someone show such extraordinary generosity. Hopefully, sooner or later they'll come to see that only *God* can relax the stranglehold that most people have on their possessions. Only He can transform a hoarding heart to a joy-filled heart that's motivated to put Jesus' words into action: "It is more blessed to give than to receive."

What might happen in the lives of your friends and family members if you relaxed your grip on your own material possessions? Think about whose heart might open up, or whose attitude might soften, or who might get curious and start asking spiritual questions, if you applied the instructions found in 1 John 3:18: "Dear children, let us not love with words or tongue but with actions and in truth."

Try God on this one. Put your faith into action on behalf of others—action that requires some investment—and watch the return He'll bring in the form of changed lives.

Modelling over the long haul

The third kind of sacrifice I'd like to discuss is a sustained, long-term effort that will affect the lives of people outside the family of God. It's the sacrifice of a consistent, godly lifestyle.

I've found that some nuts are hard to crack. Spiritual cynicism runs deep in certain people. They need to watch a Christian live out his or her faith over a substantial period of time before they'll be convinced the whole thing isn't a scam. There are more of those people around than we tend to think. They watch and keep score of our moral and spiritual consistency, often without even realising they're doing so.

This means we have to keep on living a life that backs up our words. We have to make the sacrifice of running a marathon and not merely a 100-yard dash. You know, it's not much of a trick to project a squeaky-clean Christian image to friends and colleagues for a short season. You can pump yourself up to put on a spiritual facade for a few months or maybe even a whole year.

But it's going to take longer than that to make an impact on some of the people in your world. The hardcore types inwardly smirk and say: "This too shall pass. A year from now you'll be into astrology or crystals."

Don't be surprised if this is the attitude of some of the people closest to you, including family members. They're the ones who have seen you go through all kinds of phases before: earth shoes, eccentric diets, tae kwon do classes, pyramid marketing schemes, subliminal tapes you played under your pillow each night to improve your attitude, and the like. Now you're coming along and saying, "I've found what's been missing in my life all of these years. It's Jesus Christ!" And they're thinking, "yeah, isn't that what you were saying about those herbal food supplements a couple of years ago? How long is *this* fling going to last?"

Do you see the problem? Maybe you haven't dabbled in *all* these fads, but if you're like most people, you've probably been through enough excursions in full view of these people to make them a bit calloused to the latest claims.

The question is, are you willing to prove them wrong by making the sacrifice of living a consistent, high-integrity, Christian life, not just for a season, but for the long haul?

Romans 12:1–2 days, "Offer your bodies as living sacrifices, holy and pleasing to God—which is your spiritual worship. Do not conform any longer to the pattern of this world, but be transformed by the renewing of your mind. . . ." This means that we need to have integrity in every area of our lives. It means saying "no" to evil allurements, "no" to sensual temptations, "no" to compromise, "no" to unethical opportunities for personal gain; in other words, we must consistently say "no" to sin.

There is, of course, a positive side to this, too. We need to say "yes" to righteousness and compassion and truth, even when it hurts. We need to say "yes" to God's guidance and the Bible's teachings and the Spirit's promptings.

And we must keep living out these "yes" and "no" responses day in and day out, month in and month out, year in and year out. That's a sobering thought, isn't it? It's clearly easier to *talk* about than it is to *do*! But it's an essential ingredient of contagious Christianity.

Unfortunately, the history books are full of stories of believers who burst out of the starting blocks with incredible energy and enthusiasm but who wound up being sidelined only a lap or two into the race. And this causes doubters to disbelieve all the more. They just grin, and say to each other, "See, I knew it was only a phase. Didn't I tell you the whole deal was a scam, and that it would never last?" Untold damage has been done to the cause of Christ because some people gear up for a sprint when they need to train for the marathon.

I mentioned earlier that my wife, Lynne, and I had the opportunity to spend a day with Billy and Ruth Graham. One of the memories that lingers in my mind is the realisation that these two have paid the price of Christian consistency for nearly fifty years of ministry together. That's *half a century* of being "living sacrifices". Half a century of resisting temptation, compromise, and seductions that could have put them in the ditch. Half a century of developing and expressing truth and compassion and servanthood and humility.

One of the reasons I believe God is using Billy so powerfully, especially in these later years of his ministry, is that there's a whole generation of his peers who Billy has just worn down. He's simply outlasting them! In effect, he's saying, "You know, what I told you ten years ago, and twenty years ago, and thirty years ago, and forty years ago, and fifty years ago is still as true today as it ever was. It's true in my life, and it's true in millions of other lives."

And a lot of his peers are saying, "You've made your point. I've watched you for half a century, and I'm beginning to believe it's real."

Although our actions have nothing to do with gaining our own salvation, they might be used by God to save somebody else! What we do really matters, and it can affect the eternities of people we care about.

That realisation about the Grahams reinforced to me that I'd better gear up for a marathon myself. It was good timing, too, because though I had run the beginning of my race with fairly good speed, I was getting fatigued on about the eighth mile of a twenty-six-mile marathon! I knew I needed to manage my life better so I could be a living sacrifice for the duration of the course.

How about you? Are you a sprinter or a marathon runner? Might you have some family members who are saying, "I'm going to just sit back and watch you"? Why not decide right now that with God's help you're going to wear down every cynic, scoffer, and doubter in your life?

To do this, you're going to have to maintain a high-integrity, high-compassion, high-sacrifice, godly life, day after day. You'll have to live it not just at church, but at home, at work or school, in the neighbourhood, and at the football match. Are you ready to commit today? The marathon's underway!

The impact of a Godly life

When we show sacrificial love to others in the ways I've been discussing, we're emulating the example and teaching of our leader Himself. It was Jesus who said, in John 15:12–13, "My command is this: Love each other as I have loved you. Greater love has no one than this, that one lay down his life for his friends."

It's encouraging to know that when we give part of our lives for our friends, our example makes it a lot easier for them to understand and accept the claim that Jesus gave *His* life as a sacrifice on their behalf.

The Bible says that we're saved from our sins by faith in God, apart from good works. And that's the gospel truth, isn't it? Our positive behaviour has nothing to do with obtaining salvation. It's a gift of God freely given to those who trust Him.

But something else should be added: Although our actions have nothing to do with gaining our own salvation, *they might be used by God to save somebody else!* What we do really matters, and it can affect the eternities of people we care about.

I'm sure you've seen the logic I've followed in this section. Authenticity, compassion, and sacrifice all work together to help those outside the faith come to the point of saying, "The proof is in the living, and the evidence seems irrefutable. Who else but God could make anyone so real and kind and consistent as these people are? I wonder what I need to do to have what they have?"

In terms of the salt metaphor, we've made a good start on understanding what it means to live a highly potent Christian life. But in order to have *maximum impact*, we must go on. The next issue I'll address is how we can be more strategic in achieving closer proximity to those we hope to influence for Christ. That's where the action *really* begins!

SECTION THREE

The Potential of Close Proximity

HP + *CP* + CC = MI

CHAPTER SEVEN

Strategic Opportunities in Relationships

Where do you go when you have a problem? Whom do you turn to when you need help or advice on some issue of great importance in your life? Or, for that matter, whom do you talk to when you want an opinion on what kind of new car or vacuum cleaner to buy?

Now let's look at the flipside of these questions. How do you feel when a stranger tries to talk to you about personal matters? Do you relish the thought of interacting with people you don't know about below-the-surface issues in your life?

Suppose you're spending some leisure time with your family on a Saturday morning, when suddenly your privacy is interrupted by a knock at the door. There stand two religious people who want to tell you how you can become part of God's organisation. Let me guess: You get excited and think, "Wow, a chance to talk to some articulate people about such an interesting and important topic!" Right?

I seriously doubt it. If you're like most of us, your first response is, "Oh no! Why did they have to show up *today*? I'm not in any mood to talk to people off the street about topics that are so complicated and personal—not to mention the fact that they're probably trained to argue with everything I say!"

If *you*, a Christian who's committed to spreading God's love and truth to others, feel that way when it comes to talking to strangers about spiritual matters, just think how your irreligious friends must feel in similar situations! They're likely horrified by the thought of talking to someone they don't know about their private lives.

It's no wonder that so many of the older, impersonal approaches to spreading the faith don't work very well anymore. As people in our culture have grown further and further from their Christian roots and heritage, they've become less and less comfortable talking to anyone—*especially people they don't know*—about matters of faith. With the increasing secularisation of society, there seems to be a proportionate decrease in people's willingness to move outside their comfort zones in order to search for answers to life's most crucial questions.

How much attention do you pay to all the addressed-to-Occupant junk mail that comes through your letterbox every day? It's probably safe to assume that gospel leaflets, tracts, direct mail from churches, and ads in the Yellow Pages or in the church section of the local newspaper don't get much attention either. And aren't you as sceptical as I am about whether clever slogans on Christian bumper stickers and John 3:16 banners at football matches have any meaningful affect on people? I certainly don't hear many testimonies these days from people who've been reached by these impersonal approaches.

Even the higher-quality Christian programming on radio and television, for all its expense and effort, tends to miss the truly unchurched people who need so desperately to be reached. From my interaction with these individuals, I've found that they're usually unaware that such programmes even exist.

The fact is, all of us experience discomfort when someone outside our circle of friends tries to influence us about personal, significant matters. We all naturally gravitate toward people we already know and trust. Friends listen to friends.

Please don't misunderstand me. I'm not denying that God sometimes uses these techniques to touch people with truth. Regardless of the approach, there will always be an occasional story here and there to prove that these efforts have at least some worth. I'm just saying that as people get more and more immune to impersonal methods, we'd be wise to start putting fewer of our eggs in those baskets.

The fact is, *all* of us experience discomfort when someone outside our circle of friends tries to influence us about personal, significant matters. We all naturally gravitate toward people we already know and trust. Friends listen to friends. They confide in friends. They let friends influence them. They buy from friends—and that's true of both products and ideas.

So if we're going to impact our world for Christ, the most effective approach will be through friendships with those who need to be reached. We'll have to get close to them so they can see that we genuinely care about them individually and that we have their best interests in mind. Over time, *that* will earn their trust and respect.

That's why the formula in chapter three is so important. It was built on Jesus' declaration that we are the salt of the earth and the light of the world. Looking at the first of those, we established two reasons why He used the salt metaphor. The first was that salt must have high potency (HP) to produce its intended effect. Jesus said salt that has lost its savour is worthless. That's why our last section was devoted to developing several of the characteristics that Christians need to have in order to be highly potent.

But the most powerful salt in the world has no impact when left in the shaker. And the most authentic, compassionate, and sacrificial Christians on the planet will not influence irreligious people until they make contact with them. That's why this section will key in on the second element of the formula: CP, which stands for close proximity. We'll explore the building of authentic and trusting relationships that can get us into influence-range with those who we hope to reach.

The cart before the horse

But let's be honest. The whole enterprise of developing friendships of integrity with unchurched people takes significant amounts of time and effort, not to mention some occasional discomfort. So our temptation may be to short-circuit the process and—ready or not—issue a spiritual challenge to the person. After all, we reason, there are too many people who need to be reached for us to spend a lot of time getting to know just one of them.

The problem is that what might seem to us to be a reasonable shortcut toward truth ends up being a wrong turn that derails the person's spiritual progress. Feeling pressured to take a premature step, they will likely slow down or, in some cases, even abort the whole process.

Mark learned this lesson the hard way. It happened a few years ago when our church was putting on a week-long presentation that combined contemporary music and drama to communicate Christianity to people who don't normally go to church.

He had bought four tickets for the Friday night performance, and along with his wife, Heidi, had invited another couple. But that couple cancelled at the last minute. Now it was the day of the event, and they were holding two extra tickets with no one to bring.

Mark drove home from the office that evening, and as he turned into his driveway, he saw the young couple who lived next door walking on the sidewalk in front of his house. They weren't married, had shown no inclination toward spiritual interests, and he only knew them by their first names. Still, he figured, why not give it a shot?

"Hey, Scott!" he called out. "I was wondering if you two are busy tonight. You see, I've got these extra tickets to a concert at our church." He quickly tried to dispel any stereotypes they might have and to convey that this would feature music they'd really like, that there would be professional-quality and up-to-date drama, good sound and lighting, and so on. And then he asked if they would like to go.

Push the pause button for a moment. If you think along the lines I do, you're probably admiring the confidence Mark showed in forthrightly explaining this opportunity and inviting a couple he'd barely even met. It was the kind of thing a lot of us *think* about doing but find it hard to muster the needed courage. The only problem, as he found out, was that it was probably *too* bold and *too* quick. It risked the possibility of scaring them away not only from this, but also from future chances for interaction.

Scott glanced shyly at his girlfriend for a moment and then looked at the ground. Somewhat awkwardly he finally said, "Um... thanks anyway, but I don't think we'll go this time... but, well, if you'd ever like to get together in the back garden for a barbecue, let us know."

As they walked away, Mark thought to himself, "Why didn't *I* think of that? In fact, that's the very thing I've been teaching in my evangelism seminars for years: *you've got to barbecue first*!"

It's so important that we make investments in friendships—what I sometimes call paying relational rent—in order to gain the person's trust and respect, as well as to earn the right to talk to them about spiritual issues.

Interestingly, Mark did follow up later with Scott. After a few weeks he called him and suggested that the four of them see a movie and then go out for dessert afterwards. When the night came, Mark and Heidi decided that they would not bring up topics related to church or Christianity. They knew they'd already gone too fast, and they determined to "barbecue" several times with the couple before even thinking about trying to steer the conversation into matters of faith. But to their surprise, that same night in the restaurant, Scott himself asked some questions of a spiritual nature!

Out of that experience came a maxim Mark has been teaching ever since: the "Barbecue-First Principle". It embodies the very lesson that I'm emphasising in this section. We're wise to try to first establish relationships on natural, non-threatening grounds and then later, in the context of that relationship, open up the conversation to spiritual issues. And as this story illustrates, in many cases this doesn't have to be a long wait. A lot of people are looking for a trusted confidant with whom they can discuss such important matters.

Biblical examples

To reinforce what I'm saying, let's look at the inspiring example of the life of Jesus. It's amazing how often we overlook the fact that He spent the majority of His time with those outside the religious establishment. In fact, most of His encounters with the religious people involved challenging their attitudes and illustrating to them how much lost people matter to God.

It's natural to recoil a bit and say "How could Jesus do that? What could possibly motivate the sinless Son of God to associate with such unsavoury individuals? Didn't He understand how corrupt they were?"

Time, however, tends to soften history, and the sinners Christ hung out with may seem to us more safe and sanitised than the ones who so recklessly rebel against Him today. It's easy to forget, for example, that the tax collectors He associated with really did extort large amounts of money from the downtrodden people around them, or that the prostitutes He expressed compassion for actually engaged in illicit sexual activity for pay, in the same way they do today. But that's exactly what they did. Jesus intentionally rubbed shoulders with the lowest of spiritual reprobates of His day because they mattered to Him and He wanted to lead them into the family of God.

When you let these truths soak in, it's natural to recoil a bit and say "How could Jesus do that? What could possibly motivate the sinless Son of God to associate with such unsavoury individuals? Didn't He understand how corrupt they were?"

Many of us grew up in church singing songs like, "Jesus! What a Friend for Sinners", and thinking, "that's right. I'm sure glad He's *my* friend." It all sounds good and feels good until we realise that His friendship with sinners goes much farther than just caring about us now that we're in His family. Scripture says that we love Him because He *first* loved us, when we were still disobedient rebels covered with the guilt and shame that sin inevitably brings. And He's a friend for a world full of people who are in that same condition right now.

Another role model is Paul. He said in 1 Corinthians 9:22–23, "I have become all things to all men so that by all possible means I might save some. I do all this for the sake of the gospel, that I may share in its blessings." He cared enough to inconvenience and stretch Himself in order to make contact with people and influence them toward Christ. His real challenge comes, however, in the next verse where He tells us likewise to "Run in such a way as to get the prize."

Barriers to building relationships

There are a number of stumbling blocks that keep Christians from taking up that challenge and putting effort into nourishing relationships with nonbelievers in their world. Let's look at some of those obstacles:

Biblical issues

Some of us were raised repeatedly hearing verses that stressed, "Friendship with the world is hatred toward God," and "not of the world," and "Come out from among them and be separate." If these verses were integral to your Christian upbringing, the very idea of befriending irreligious people probably sounds questionable and maybe even unbiblical.

Let's deal with this idea briefly by looking a little closer at the Bible passages themselves. First, James 4:4 does say that we are not to be friends with this world.

But it's clear from other passages, such as 1 John 2:15–17, that the word "world" is not referring to the people themselves, but to the sin and evil that people in the world commit. In other words, we must follow Christ's command to love others without falling into the sin of loving or participating in the bad things they do. As James 1:27 puts it, we need to keep ourselves "from being polluted by the world."

Similarly John 17:14, where Jesus says that we are not of this world, is sometimes interpreted that we should not associate with people outside God's family. But verses 15–18 demonstrate the opposite: "My prayer is not that you take them out of the world but that you protect them from the evil one.... As you sent me into the world, I have sent them into the world." And why was Jesus sent into the world? According to His own confession, it was "to seek and to save what was lost" (Luke 19:10).

Jesus was accused by His enemies of being a "friend of tax collectors and 'sinners' " (Luke 7:34). Though this was meant to be a derogatory term, Jesus never denied it. Instead, He took it as a compliment and actively embodied it.

And what about the admonition to "come out from them...and be separate"? This comes from 2 Corinthians 6:17, where Paul is concluding his warning to believers to avoid situations where they are "yoked" with unbelievers. This clearly does not refer to everyday friendships, but to more formal alliances, which often prove to be spiritually harmful to the Christian. In fact,

Paul said in his earlier letter to the same church that ordinary interaction with non-Christians is all right and even necessary (1 Corinthians 5:9–10).

We can conclude by reminding ourselves that Jesus was accused by His enemies of being a "friend of tax collectors and 'sinners' " (Luke 7:34). Though this was meant to be a derogatory term, Jesus never denied it. Instead, He took it as a compliment and actively embodied it.

Spiritual Danger

So we've seen that the idea of getting up close to irreligious people for spiritual purposes is a biblical enterprise modelled by Jesus and Paul. But what about the risks associated with being around those who are actively rebelling against God? And what did Paul have in mind in 1 Corinthians 15:33 when he said, "Do not be misled: 'Bad company corrupts good character' "?

First the verse. When read in context, it becomes clear that Paul was specifically warning against accepting religious teachers who deny the resurrection of Christ. He was saying, "Don't let their scepticism on this issue lead you astray. The fact that Jesus literally rose from the dead is central and indispensable to the Christian faith."

More broadly, there seems to be a general principle implied here. Namely, when we associate with someone who believes something other than the true gospel message, we need to make certain *we're* the one whose influence is prevailing.

Another way of putting this is that we need to be on the offense rather than the defense. We need to be ready to bring God's truth to bear on any situation in which we find ourselves. Or, as Paul said, to "demolish arguments and every pretension that sets itself up against the knowledge of God, and . . . take captive every thought to make it obedient to Christ" (2 Corinthians 10:4, 5).

This means that when we sense that we're being negatively influenced by the ideas and actions of the other person, it's time to back away, at least for a while. It's critical that we remain the dominant influence in moral and spiritual matters. In many situations, this is not as difficult as it might sound. When we approach friendships with a purpose—to contagiously influence people for Christ—we'll be more likely to persevere in upholding what is morally right and true.

I find myself thinking, "What am I doing here? The voices are loud, the language is foul, the egos are out of control. Why am I here?" And often the gentle whisper of the Holy Spirit says to me, "You're doing the kind of thing that Jesus did."

Risking your reputation

"But if I start spending personal time in public places with pagans," you might say, "what will the people in my church think?" That's a valid concern worth putting on the table because *some* of the Christians you know will probably misunderstand your efforts to relate to irreligious people.

You're in good company, though, because Jesus not only *risked* His reputation with the religious community, He *ruined* it! In Luke 7:34 we read that they accused Jesus of being a glutton and a drunkard. While He was clearly neither, the fact that these people thought He was tells us a lot about the kinds of individuals with whom He spent time.

In Matthew 9:12–13, Jesus said that He associated with sinners because they are like sick people who need a doctor. The danger was, and still is, of course, that a doctor may be mistakenly identified as one of the patients.

We looked earlier at Luke 15:3–32, the passage where Jesus illustrated how much wayward people matter to God by presenting three parables: the lost sheep, the lost coin, and the prodigal son. We've discussed the lesson but not the reason Jesus went to such lengths to drive it home. When you look at the first two verses of the chapter, His motivation becomes clear.

Jesus was responding to the religious leaders who were muttering to each other about how inappropriate it was for Him to associate with such disreputable people. Jesus wanted them to know that not only was it not wrong, it was well worth the effort because of the value God places on lost people.

Personal discomfort

Let's just admit it: It's hard to go back into close proximity with the kinds of people we used to run with. Their language makes us uncomfortable, their humour is off-colour and embarrassing, and their wayward values and activities leave us wondering if the spiritual gap is just too wide to bridge. You may have only recently escaped that environment. So your natural reaction may be, "And now you're telling me to go back into it?"

My answer to that question is, well, yes and no. We certainly don't want to go back to *stay* in that environment. But we do need to *visit* it for the sake of the people who still live there, who God loves, and who we've got to care about. But yes, it will feel awkward at times.

I referred earlier to my enjoyment of sailboat racing. My crew is made up of nine guys, and they're not the kind of group you'd likely encounter at the Sunday school picnic.

Sailing protocol requires the boat owners and crews to gather at the yacht club after each regatta to verify the race results, settle any protests, and to receive the prizes for first, second, and third place.

I'll give you three guesses what everyone does while the race committee is doing it's work. You're right: they consume alcoholic beverages in massive quantities. I can't tell you how many times I've stood in a circle of eight to ten mildly inebriated sailors as they argued endlessly about who had the best spinnaker launch or the best windward leg.

I find myself thinking, "What am *I* doing here? The voices are loud, the language is foul, the egos are out of control. Why am I here?" And often the gentle whisper of the Holy Spirit says to me, "You're building bridges. You're establishing trust. You're laying the groundwork for conversations that might happen a year from now. You're doing the kind of thing that Jesus did."

The kinds and levels of discomfort we'll encounter in building relationships with unbelievers will vary, but God will help us face them and honour our efforts in the process. And it'll all be worth it.

Making it personal

Can I suggest that you do something that will take this discussion out of the theoretical and into the practical? Write down the names of three people whose lives you'd like to impact spiritually. These should be individuals within your sphere of influence who you feel you have some chance of eventually talking with about Christ.

Making this "Impact List" will help you move away from hoping to someday, somehow reach some nameless, faceless seekers, and into specific action aimed at helping three people you know and care about.

It's important to ask God for guidance in choosing the names. And you need to keep talking to Him about them, asking the Holy Spirit to open them up to the love and truth of Christ. Also, pray that God will help you express unconditional love and no-strings-attached friendship, as well as give you wisdom on how to approach them and what to say about Him.

I like the way it's been said by my friend, Dieter Zander: "We need to talk to God about people, *then* talk to people about God." Keep in mind that the Holy Spirit wants to be your unseen partner in reaching your friends, family members, coworkers, and neighbours with Christ's life-giving gospel message. It's important to turn to Him for wisdom and power every step along the way.

Let me end this chapter with a word of encouragement. You can't be a contagious Christian without getting close enough to other people to let them catch the disease. This is where the whole enterprise is won or lost, at the actual point of contact. As I said earlier, friends listen to real friends. *So become one.* If we don't start there, we can't effectively get anywhere.

Later on we're going to talk about ways to clearly communicate the content of your faith, but it's important to recognise now that no amount of preparation will do you any good if you haven't made contact.

And what's exciting is that when you're part of a strategic friendship, you'll find out it can really be fun. You'll see your faith deepening, your relational world expanding, and your reliance on God growing. It's like I've been telling you—it's an incredible adventure!

CHAPTER EIGHT

Rubbing Shoulders with Irreligious People

Parties. I grew up with two different kinds, each quite unlike the other.

The first type was the gathering of the *religious ranks*. If you were raised in a Christian setting, you'll probably remember the post-service fellowship get-togethers where everyone knew everybody. Friendly, familial joking and chatting along with that church-basement ambiance. The faint but familiar aroma of coffee, crayons, cologne, and cleaning supplies. Red punch. There always had to be plenty of red punch, but never with quite enough sugar. Shuffleboard floors. Folding chairs. The sound of someone plunking on the piano in a side room. And kids everywhere. You get the picture.

The other variety was the out-of-control assemblage of the *renegade ranks*. This was the born-to-be-wild, party-till-you-drop, you-only-go-around-once crowd. The alcohol flowed freely, the talk was cheap, the music was turned up to the point of distortion. Some came to have fun, others to fit in, and those who could do neither would generally just fake it.

My growing up years were spent at the parties of the religious ranks. Later, during high school, I had my share of exposure to the parties of the renegade ranks.

But one thing I don't remember ever seeing were get-togethers that mixed members of the two crowds together—at least, not on purpose. It might have happened occasionally, like at wedding receptions, but when it did it was always uncomfortable. To avoid a clash, the two groups would ignore each other and celebrate among themselves until later into the night, when the renegade group gradually took over and scared the religious people away.

Matthew's party

The situation wasn't much different in the first century, and that's what made Matthew's actions seem so outrageous. You can read about them in Luke 5:29. In short, Matthew threw a banquet and did the unheard-of. He invited both his religious *and* his irreligious buddies. It was an intentionally mixed crowd—a party with a purpose.

You've got to give him credit. Matthew had become a Christian while pursuing a career as a tax collector, which, in those days, was about one notch above being part of the mob. People in his profession were notorious for pilfering money from the poor. If you were a tax collector, you essentially had a license to extort.

But his encounter with Jesus radically transformed his heart. As a result, he had an immediate concern for his friends who were not yet committed to Christ. His natural desire was to help them find what he'd found. The only real question was, how? He hadn't been through an evangelism seminar. He hadn't graduated from a seminary. He lacked printed materials. All he had was a grace-filled heart and a determined spirit. He'd figure it out.

One strategy would be to bring his tax-collecting colleagues to the temple to hear someone who was more articulate in explaining spiritual truth. But the only option there was a robed rabbi reading Old Testament law. It didn't take Matthew long to realise that approach wouldn't connect very well with these high-flying, risk-taking, card-carrying pagans.

He could have just given up. He might have wrung his hands and said, "Well, there are no good options. The robed rabbi plan is out, and Jesus' teaching ministry is too spontaneous and unscheduled. Besides, they probably wouldn't go out of their way to hear someone preaching on a hillside. And I'm certainly not qualified. I guess I'll just have to let them fend for themselves."

You know, there are a lot of Christians who wring their hands and insulate their hearts from the plight of their lost friends and family members. But Matthew wasn't willing to do that. Instead, he persisted. I'm sure he must have thought hard about it, prayed for wisdom and direction, and perhaps asked his believing friends for their advice.

Then he had an idea: he'd throw a party. Of course! His buddies *loved* parties; *big* parties, and the more the merrier.

Now all he had to do was figure out a way to inject his primary purpose into this party. So he asked Jesus and the disciples if they'd be willing to come along to plant some spiritual seeds here and there in the hopes of something significant taking root in his friends' hearts.

On the night of the event, only heaven knows what strategic conversations took place. We don't have many details, except that the Pharisees got wind of it and didn't like it. They apparently thought that Jesus and the disciples were doing evangelism the wrong way, so they pulled them aside and challenged them for socialising with such unsavoury characters. Frankly, I think part of their problem was that they thought everyone was having too much fun.

During this exchange with the Pharisees, I can picture freshly converted Matthew listening in and wondering if he'd done the right thing. After all, this was his first evangelistic effort, and now Jesus was getting chewed out by the religious brass. I can imagine him thinking, *Maybe I should have just dragged my friends to the temple. Or perhaps I should have just walked away and not tried anything. Now everybody's upset. Jesus is getting the third degree. I'd better not take any more risks like this one. I'll leave evangelism to the professionals.*

Unconventional approaches that strategically mix the spiritual haves and have-nots are not merely acceptable, they are essential to God's redemptive efforts.

But then all of a sudden he heard Jesus defending his actions! Jesus commended Matthew's party idea by reminding the Pharisees that sick people are the ones who need a doctor. What good is it, He chided, for doctors to spend their time hanging around with healthy people? In other words, unconventional approaches that strategically mix the spiritual haves and have-nots are not merely acceptable, they are *essential* to God's redemptive efforts.

Though the text doesn't give details on what happened next, I can imagine Jesus, after answering the Pharisees, turning and putting His arm on Matthew's shoulder.

"Good job, Matthew," I think He may have said. "I understand your motivation behind what's happening here. You assessed you friends' spiritual needs and you looked at your options for meeting those needs, and then you got creative. You took some risks. I want you to know, Matthew, that I love your ideas and I love your heart for lost people. And I'm honoured to be a part of your plan to reach them. Now, let's get back to the party!"

Learning from Matthew's example

If I'm right about this, then there are principles here that apply just as much to us today. I think God's desire is for us to value unbelieving friends the way Matthew did. I also think that He would want us to be wary of status quo techniques for evangelising lost people, when in our hearts we know these aren't the best solutions for reaching the people we hope to help. And He certainly doesn't want us to wring our hands over the dilemma and give up.

I think God would challenge us to do what Matthew did. Be innovative. Think creatively. Within the parameters of biblical principles, come up with a strategy that is true to who we are and to who our friends are. Pray hard and be willing to go out on a limb. Learn from mistakes and adjust the approach accordingly.

And along the way, remember to focus on people rather than programmes. The action starts when you make contact with another human being. Salt must touch something to have its effect; likewise, the doctor has to find ways to spend time with people who need his services. You've got to seize opportunities to rub shoulders with irreligious people if you're going to reach anybody.

Contagious Christianity is friend-to-friend, person-to-person, neighbour-to-neighbour. The plan is biblical, it's logical, it's strategic, and it was proven by Jesus, Paul, Matthew, and many others since. The remaining question is, "How do I take the first step? What can I do to get close to unbelievers in the hope of eventually leading them to Christ?"

I want to respond by looking at practical ways you can reach out to three groups of people in your world: people you know, people you used to know, and people you'd like to know.

People you know

There's a common misconception that the most vital and meaningful approach to evangelism involves making contact with people we don't know. But exactly the opposite is true. It's the people we *do* know who have already developed a measure of trust in us and our motives, and are therefore most in range of influence. To the degree that we've developed a contagious character like we discussed in section two, our acquaintances will be attracted to who we are and the faith that we represent. They may not come out and say so, but attributes like authenticity, compassion, and sacrifice are powerful magnets to those who observe them in your life.

But the key element missing in so many of these relationships is relaxed time together outside of the routines of work, household chores, or the everyday busyness of life. We simply need more "down time" in order to allow conversations to deepen into the real, personal issues of life. How can we take steps to ensure that happens? Let's examine two possible approaches. The first one works through planned events, and the second through more informal means.

Throw a "Matthew Party"

Social events strategically designed to mix selected members of the "religious ranks" and the "renegade ranks", or, as they've become known around our church, "Matthew Parties", can take virtually any shape or size.

They're usually designed to fulfil a modest purpose: to provide a neutral setting where contagious Christians can make low-key contact with irreligious people. These are ideal environments for strengthening existing relationships as well as cultivating new ones. And they're great places to plant some spiritual seeds and strike up conversations about matters of faith.

God's desire is for us to value unbelieving friends the way Matthew did. I also think that He would want us to be wary of status quo techniques for evangelising lost people, when in our hearts we know these aren't the best solutions for reaching the people we hope to help.

Wheels may start turning that can, over time, result in a whole new eternity for many of the people you've invited. You'll be surprised by how quickly some of them will open up and take significant spiritual steps in the direction of Christianity.

Let's look at some examples:

Golfing events

I know some people who organise golf clinics and outings for this purpose. They use them simply to deepen their friendships with unchurched acquaintances, though, to their surprise, one time a woman they'd invited ended up praying to receive Christ right there at the driving range!

Holiday parties
Russ and Lynette, a couple from our church, annually host a fourth of July party at their home. They invite just about everyone they know—Christian and non-Christian—for the dual purpose of having fun and exposing their unbelieving friends to believers. They set up grills and outdoor games in their garden, along with a big awning and some tables and chairs, and just let people roam freely in and out of the house. The most spiritual thing they do is have contemporary Christian music playing over the stereo. But by the end of the day, some strategic friendships have been started, and a lot of lost people have seen Christians enjoying themselves and interacting with others. A number of them have also received a warm invitation to visit one of our church's weekend services.

Contagious Christianity is friend-to-friend, person-to-person, neighbour-to-neighbour. The plan is biblical, it's logical, it's strategic, and it was proven by Jesus, Paul, Matthew, and many others since.

Events for children on the street
Natalie enjoys hosting Matthew parties of a different kind. One was a fairly elaborate carnival sponsored for the children in her neighbourhood. She brought in clowns, organised games, put up decorations, and invited members from our church's evangelism team to help her run the event, which was creatively tailored to fit her interests and those of the people she hoped to reach.

Pie parties

A friend of mine recently noticed that a new family was moving into a home on his street. He commented to his wife that they ought to do something to reach out and welcome them. She said, "Okay, let's have a pie party."

"How does that work?" he asked.

"Simple. I'll invite them to come over Friday night, and you pick up a pie on the way home from work."

She did and he did, and that began a process of developing a genuine friendship that is gradually opening up to spiritual interaction.

Baptism receptions

A newer Christian named Jim was about to be baptised. He decided to maximise the event in the tradition of Matthew by printing invitations and sending them to friends and family members of every religious background. He even organised and paid for a meal at an area hotel for all who responded to his RSVP request.

His investment paid off. The guest list included relatives who flew in from long distances away as well as acquaintances who drove to the church from all over the area. During the meal afterwards, Jim stood up and thanked them all for coming, and then in a simple but direct way, he told the story of how he'd decided to follow Christ and what that meant. His words spoke volumes to those in attendance and resulted in further conversations about spiritual things.

I know another couple who organise spiritually strategic tennis tournaments. Others sponsor football or other games in the park. Some use camping or backpacking trips. Still more go on sailing excursions. Street parties and even simple garden barbecues can be effective. We could go on and on, because the sky's the limit. You name it, and there's probably a creative way to utilise it in putting together a Matthew Party.

So can I issue you a challenge? If you've been wringing your hands wondering what you could do to raise your proximity level with people who need Christ, why not brainstorm some new ideas with a few like-minded friends? Dream a little. Pray together about it. Then take a risk and see what God does.

Involve others in your everyday activities

Another misconception many of us have is that in order to build relationships with irreligious people, we'll have to add a lot of new activities to our already overburdened schedules.

Well, you'll be glad to know that it's not true. An effective way to maximise those friendships is to invite the person to join you in the things you're already planning to do. Here are some examples:

Sharing a meal

You eat just about every day, don't you? How about inviting a non-Christian coworker out for lunch now and then, or asking the unbelieving neighbours to meet you in your back garden for a barbecue?

Watching the game

Maybe you're a sports fan and plan to watch an important game. Why not get out of the rut of watching them alone or with safe Christian company, and mix it up with a few men or women from your street? Sure, you might hear some bad language when the other team scores, but they might see some positive values in your home that will attract them toward Christ.

Sporting activities

What about recreational activities? Golf, tennis, football, cricket, skiing, cycling, riding, fishing, hiking—the list is endless. If it's an activity you'll do anyway, why not do it with some company that may benefit spiritually?

Exercise time

The health club is a good place to build on existing friendships as well as form new ones. Why not meet a coworker or acquaintance from down the street to lift weights or do aerobics?

A board member of our church who is now one of my closest friends came to Christ, in part, because we played squash together during the time he was investigating Christianity. We'd go swing away at the ball for an hour, yell at each other, push each other around, and then have a good talk in the sauna afterwards. By the time we went home, we'd had a couple of hours together building our relationship and addressing his questions about the faith. Eventually he committed his life to Christ.

Babysitting and work exchanges

Relationships with those next door can be deepened by taking turns watching each other's children. Not only do you save the money you would have paid a sitter, your neighbour's children will have a chance to see a Christian family in action. You might also help each other with everyday tasks like moving furniture, planting shrubs, or changing the oil in your cars.

Children's activities

Another idea is to get together with the families of your childrens' friends for games, school programmes, or field trips.

Strategic workdays

The workplace is a natural environment for turning acquaintances into friendships, and friendships into spiritual opportunities. There's obviously no shortage of spiritually needy people in most fields of business. The trick is to resist becoming overwhelmed by the numbers of lost people or the depths of their disobedience to God. My advice is to avoid concentrating on the one hundred. Instead, focus on the two or three with whom you have some affinity. Then start by spending some quality time with them.

You can add to this list of examples from your own situations and interests. What's important is that you plan get-togethers that are natural for both you and your friends.

People you used to know

This is another often overlooked group with great possibility. I'm referring to people from your past with whom you've lost contact.

Few people make an effort to stay in contact with their acquaintances once they leave school, a job, or a neighbourhood. Even friendships that were relatively close tend to dissolve within a year or two after one of the parties moves away. Generally, the older people get, the less seriously they take parting comments like, "Oh, don't worry, we'll stay in touch." They say to themselves, "Yeah, right. I've heard that one before, and it hasn't happened yet!"

So when you actually do write or call a former coworker or classmate, he or she will be pleasantly surprised and open to the idea of getting together to catch up. What makes this opportunity so exciting is that there's a built-in curiosity factor on both sides to know how the other person has grown or changed.

Because of this curiosity factor, the person doesn't even have to have been a close friend. Mark, for instance, ran into Kirk, an old high school classmate he'd graduated with more than ten years earlier in their home town a thousand miles away. And although they had barely known each other back then, they were both glad to find a familiar face in their new town. They enjoyed getting together to reminisce about the people, classes, and events they both knew. And it was fun to catch up on who had done what, gone where, and married whom.

Mark soon discovered a spiritual oneness in Kirk, and they had some significant conversations about important issues. Things really took off when Mark, with the help of a mutual friend, helped Kirk and his wife, Kim, find a good church in the area they lived in. They got involved, grew in their faith, and are now looking for ways to reach out and encourage others.

A newer Christian in our church named Kathy took our evangelism course and became excited about reaching out to others. Out of the blue she decided to call a friend named Rae Ann who she'd hardly seen in twenty years. It turned out to be providential timing, because Rae Ann's husband was in the hospital dying of a terminal illness, and she didn't have anyone to turn to for support.

If you've been wringing your hands wondering what you could do to raise your proximity level with people who need Christ, why not brainstorm some new ideas with a few like-minded friends? Dream a little. Pray together about it. Then take a risk and see what God does.

Kathy felt sad for her friend but excited about the opportunity to be used by God to love and encourage both of them, which she did wholeheartedly. In the process, she and Rae Ann became close again, and Kathy was able to help both of them put their trust in Christ. Though Rae Ann's husband died within a few weeks, she had newfound hope that she'd see him in heaven. Shortly thereafter, Kathy and Rae Ann were baptised together. And it all started with a phone call to an old friend.

Who could you call? What address do you need to look up so you can drop a note of encouragement and re-establish a waiting-to-be-recovered friendship? Even if you've lost track of where the person lives, a little creative thinking and a couple of calls can usually get you the information you'll need.

Call them out of curiosity. Call them for fun. But in the process, prayerfully watch for opportunities to inject into the conversation some of the changes God has affected in your life. They'll probably be more interested than you'd expect.

People you'd like to know

Now we've come to the category that makes a lot of Christians nervous. Talking to people they know or even going back to re-establish old relationships doesn't sound too bad. But trying to talk to strangers about God? That's going a bit too far.

Relax. We're not talking about spiritually accosting unsuspecting passersby! The idea is to find ways to build rapport with people you come into contact with through natural means, with the hopes of eventually being able to discuss spiritual topics. I even have a fancy title for it: strategic consumerism.

Strategic consumerism

Here's how it works. All of us go to garages, restaurants, dry cleaners, grocery stores, clothing shops, and other places for the necessities of everyday life, right? Well, with a little forethought, those mundane errands can be turned into evangelistic adventures.

The first step is to approach the people working in these places not as objects to serve us but as people who matter to God and who are worthy of our love and concern. That's the fundamental attitude necessary for *every* aspect of contagious Christianity.

When we approach individuals with that attitude, and when we frequent their place of business with courtesy and concern for their welfare, it's pretty easy to get on a friendly first-name basis. The relationship will grow as we show genuine interest in their life, their family, their work, and their hobbies. Over time, we'll begin to earn their trust and pique their curiosity about what it is that makes us different from so many other customers who don't seem to care about them at all. In other words, the combination of high potency and close proximity will make you into some very effective salt.

I've developed a friendship in this way that has added a new dimension to my visits to a particular restaurant and that may one day serve to turn another wayward person toward Christ. It's a place my son, Todd, and I like to frequent. Over the course of time, we've made friends with the man who runs the place.

He's kind of a gruff man, and one day he commented to me that he couldn't wait for the weekend, when he was going to do some real living. "I'm curious," I said. "What exactly *is* real living?"

"A day on my powerboat with a case of beer, a carton of cigarettes, and my girl in a bikini—*that's* real living," he enthusiastically replied.

"You don't know what real living is," I retorted. "Real living is a sail boat and a steady wind, the sun on your back, and a few close buddies you can open up your life to about things that really matter."

Events as simple as having lunch or playing golf with someone who needs to know Christ could start a process that ends up—well, that never ends at all!

"You've got to be kidding," he jeered. "That's not real living. You don't even know what real living is!"

That short exchange has put some fun into our casual but growing friendship. Each time I go in there now we end up saying to each other, "I know what real living is—and you don't!" I'm hoping one day there'll be an opportunity to deepen our interactions and, eventually, to introduce him to the One who'll show him what life is *really* all about. In the meantime, Todd and I will keep on seizing chances to dine out with a purpose.

Mark tells a similar story about his experience in a restaurant he frequents. It's a small, family-run operation, where it was easy to get on a first-name basis with the owners, a man named Steve, and his wife, Maggie.

After eating there a number of times, Maggie began to open up somewhat, and seemed to take a special interest in hearing about Mark's two children, Emma Jean and Matthew. Then one day after asking about them, she said abruptly, "I lost my baby last week!" Fighting back tears, she turned to walk away.

When Mark stopped her and asked her about it, she told him she had been pregnant but had miscarried, for the second time. Her vulnerability served to quickly deepen the friendship as Mark tried to comfort her.

A few months later when Mark stopped in for lunch, Maggie walked up to him and, with a mixture of hope and fear on her face, told him she was pregnant again.

After congratulating her, he did something that surprised even him. Acting on what seemed to be a prompting from the Holy Spirit, he told her quietly that he was going to pray for her, right there at the restaurant's front counter.

"Don't worry," he said. "It'll be short. And if anyone walks up, I'll stop." Then, without giving her time to get nervous about it, he bowed his head and said a quick, uninterrupted prayer, asking God to protect both her and the baby inside of her.

Maggie, who is a member of a non-Christian religion, was visibly touched by the gesture, and in the ensuing months told Mark when she saw him how encouraging that prayer had been. In fact, she said she was telling all of her friends about how he had prayed for her baby. As you might imagine, he was now even *more* motivated to intercede on behalf of that child! And a few months later, a healthy baby boy was born to Steve and Maggie.

When Mark called her at the hospital the next day, she made sure he knew that during a difficult part of the birthing process she had turned to God for His strength and help, and that He had come through for her!

Maggie may not be a committed Christian yet, but she's closer than ever before. And it all started with a contagious Christian stopping in a restaurant for a bite to eat.

Do these stories give you a new perspective on some of your own daily routines? How might you be able to turn ordinary activities into Spirit-directed adventures? It can all start with the practice of strategic consumerism. Or it can begin with whatever variation on the theme you'd like to give it: strategic recreation, strategic community involvements, strategic political activity and so on. Whatever the arena, Colossians 4:5 again reminds each of us to "be wise in the way you act toward outsiders; make the most of every opportunity."

Events as simple as having lunch or playing golf with someone who needs to know Christ could start a process that ends up—well, that *never* ends at all! What a privilege it is to be used by God to make contact with people for the purpose of spiritually impacting their lives in ways that last not just for this lifetime, but *forever*.

CHAPTER NINE

Finding the Approach that Fits You

This was the end. He'd written off personal evangelism and was ready to invest his time and energy elsewhere. It wasn't that he didn't believe in it anymore. He knew it was important, biblical, and the only hope for helping people find Christ. Clearly, it was something *somebody* ought to be doing. But not him. Not anymore.

What had soured my friend's attitude toward spreading the faith? He'd had a heavy dose of reaching out in ways that didn't fit him.

You see, he'd signed up for a summer-long tour of duty helping a church with evangelism. He loved that church, enjoyed the people he was partnering with, and became enthralled with some of the conversations he had with spiritual seekers along the way. The problem, however, had to do with the approach that their group employed.

The primary way they tried to spread the message was through a direct, cold-contact, knock-at-the-door-and-talk-fast-before-they-close-it methodology. They also handed out church invitations and gospel pamphlets to individuals on the street—people who often made it clear they weren't interested.

At the end of their eight-week effort, the only person who had received Christ was the brother of a woman from the church. His name was Tony, and they'd met at a dinner at Tony's sister's home. He and my friend hit it off naturally, and through the friendship that developed, the gospel was communicated and a commitment was made.

When summer ended and my friend returned home, he was thankful he had signed up but was glad it was over. Evangelism, he concluded, is for people with a certain kind of personality and temperament, a kind he clearly didn't have.

Ironically, a year later we hired him at Willow Creek Community Church to direct our evangelism ministries, a role he's fulfilled since 1987. I'm talking about Mark Mittelberg, the co-author of this book. His life's passion is leading people to Christ and teaching others how to do the same.

What happened during that year? What did Mark discover that caused such a change in his attitude? He learned he could be effective in spreading the message of Jesus Christ without trying to fit into someone else's mould. He found out he could be himself.

Menacing misconceptions

After spending many years helping seekers come to faith, I've been fascinated to find that one of the biggest barriers to effective outreach is the problem of misconceptions. And that's true on both sides of the evangelism equation.

On the seeker side, the misguided ideas people have about God's character and His church preclude them from making an open and honest spiritual search. Their inaccurate image of God and what serving Him would be like pushes them away from Him.

But when people's mistaken notions of God's nature are replaced by an accurate understanding of His grace-filled and compassionate heart, they become much more open to trusting Christ. And when they discover the acceptance, joy, and purpose that come from being part of a biblically functioning body of believers, they'll be drawn in even further.

On the believer side of the equation, misconceptions about the outreach enterprise itself tend to inhibit people from getting involved. In fact, I'm convinced that one of the greatest impediments to individuals in churches getting active in personal evangelism is that many Christians misunderstand what it actually entails. The dreaded "E Word" fills them with fear and guilt.

To illustrate the kinds of perception problem I'm referring to, let me call in one of my key witnesses: *You*.

I'd like to know what image comes to your mind when you think of the word "evangelist". Does it evoke enthusiasm for reaching your irreligious friends and family members? Or do you, like most of us, have some negative associations that come to mind with the mere mention of the word?

I've asked this question in enough groups to know that on hearing the words "evangelism" or "evangelist", many people immediately conjure up memories of infamous televangelists, known primarily for extracting large amounts of money from their well-meaning followers. Or they think of the stereotypical street preacher, megaphone in hand, blaring out barely intelligible indictments about the end of the world and the impending judgment of God.

Admittedly, many people do have a few positive images of evangelism. But the fact that so many individuals make such unflattering associations points to the immensity of the problem.

In fact, *The Day America Told the Truth*, a book by

James Patterson and Peter Kim, reports that when a national survey asked respondents to rank various professions for their honesty and integrity, TV evangelists came out almost at the very bottom, below lawyers, politicians, car salesmen, and even prostitutes. Out of the seventy-three occupations compared in this integrity rating, only two ended up lower on the scale: organised crime bosses and drug dealers! Fair or unfair, it's easy to understand why so many of us struggle with our perceptions at this point. We want to honour God by directing those around us toward His love and truth, but we wonder what we'll have to become in the process.

I'm convinced that one of the greatest impediments to individuals in churches getting active in personal evangelism is that many Christians misunderstand what it actually entails. The dreaded "E Word" fills them with fear and guilt.

Has this problem affected you? Has your passion for communicating your faith been dampened by the thought that you'll have to become something that's contrary to your own personality? Or have you, like Mark, tried to adopt an evangelism style that doesn't fit you at all?

This kind of thinking is a tragedy for the church. And it's even worse for lost people. In fact, I believe it originated as a satanic scheme to defeat the expansion of the Kingdom of God. And while it's been an extremely successful strategy, it's time for the church to put a stop to it. How can we do this? By understanding the great news that's both freeing and empowering: *God knew what He was doing when He made you.* He did! He custom-designed you with your unique combination of personality, temperament, talents, and background, and He wants to harness and use these in His mission to reach this messed-up world.

That means He wants to use you in a fashion that fits the person He made you to be. God doesn't call us all to spread His truth in the same way. Instead, He built diversity into the fabric of His body of believers. And until we realise that, we'll find ourselves needlessly imitating each other's outreach efforts, wastefully duplicating some approaches while harmfully squelching others.

Letting it look like you

So, you may be wondering, what exactly did Mark learn that so transformed his outlook on evangelism? Well, he had been attending our church's midweek worship services where I was teaching a series called, "Adventures in Personal Evangelism". On one of those nights I explained a pattern I'd noticed of how characters in the Bible took differing approaches, or styles, to communicating their faith to others.

God custom-designed you with your unique combination of personality, temperament, talents, and background, and He wants to harness and use these in His mission to reach this messed-up world.

That was new information to Mark. It opened his eyes to the fact that there's no one "right way" to spread the gospel message. And, in particular, he heard about an approach Paul used that seemed to fit him well.

The message Mark heard that night unlocked the door to his future involvement in spreading the faith. He felt free. He discovered what I hope will be liberating news to you, too: *that you can be yourself!* And, in the process, you'll be able to have maximum spiritual impact on others.

Starting with the individual

A common mistake in many arenas is to look at a need and then find a person to fill it. For example, in the world of business, people are routinely hired to fill positions not because they have any passion for that particular area, but because they meet the minimal qualifications to get the task done. In education, students frequently choose university degree programmes not because they really care about the subject matter, but because projected market demand seems to dictate it. And in churches, teachers are often chosen to instruct the Sunday school classes not because they necessarily love and care about children, but because they're willing and available.

Is it any wonder that these institutions struggle so much with absenteeism and high turnover? After any initial enthusiasm wears off, the person feels misplaced and begins to burn out.

Starting with the need and plugging people in is not a good way to develop long-term careers or passion-driven lifestyles. And this is certainly true when it comes to motivating Christians to spread the message of Christ. Yet most of the evangelism and missions appeals I hear are pitched just that way: "There's a world of hurting and lost people out there, and God needs you to sign up for our programme to help them."

But if, as it says in 1 Corinthians 12:11, the Holy Spirit really distributes spiritual gifts to each person, "just as he determines," then perhaps we can rely more on His work and turn our procedure around. Why not start with each individual believer and try to help him or her discover what kind of role God has designed for him or her to fill?

Let's look at the way God equipped six people in the New Testament to fulfil differing outreach needs. In the process, we'll discover six biblical styles of evangelism. As I describe each one, ask yourself if it might fit you.

Peter's confrontational approach

It's no secret that Peter was a "Ready-Fire-Aim" kind of guy. Whatever he did, he did it unhesitantly and with full force. When Jesus asked the disciples in Matthew 16:15 who they thought He was, Peter didn't mince words; he declared flat-out that Jesus was the Messiah. Then a few verses later he challenged Jesus' stated mission head on. Can you imagine trying to correct the Son of God? You might, if you have a confrontational style yourself!

When Peter was in the fishing boat and wanted to be with Jesus, he didn't hesitate to do whatever it took to get close to Him, even if it meant trying to walk on water. And when their enemies came to take Jesus away, Peter was ready to cut off their heads.

All Peter needed was to be convinced he was right, and there was almost no stopping him. He was direct, he was bold, and he was right to the point.

Is it any wonder God chose him as his spokesman on the day of Pentecost in Acts 2? It was a perfect fit! God needed someone unafraid to take a stand, right there in Jerusalem, the city where Jesus had been crucified a few weeks earlier. He wanted to let the thousands of people who were there know in no uncertain terms that they'd crucified the Messiah, and that they needed to call on Him for His mercy and forgiveness.

Peter's personality was custom-designed to fill the bill. With the empowerment of the Holy Spirit, he stood quite naturally and confronted the people with the facts. And God miraculously used his efforts: three thousand people trusted Christ and were baptised that same day.

As exciting as that historical event was, we need to turn our focus to today. Do you realise that there are a lot of people in your world who won't come to Christ until someone like Peter holds their feet to the fire?

I have a friend who for years played church and pretended to be a Christian. He'd heard lots of good teaching, knew the gospel message inside and out, and could quote numerous Bible verses. The only thing he lacked was a confrontational evangelist who could get in his face about his need to start living the truth he knew. Then one day God sent one. This man looked my friend in the eye and told him he was a hypocrite.

That made him angry, but it made him think. And within a week's time he'd committed his life to Christ, a decision that has transformed his life over the last twenty years.

Some people are just waiting for a contagious Christian who won't beat around the bush, but who'll clarify the truth of Christ and challenge them to do something about it. Could that Christian be you? Do you resonate with Peter's approach, or are you ready to move on to the other five options?

Actually, this is the style that's most natural for me. It's not hard for me to look people directly in the eye and ask them where they stand. I enjoy confronting and exhorting those in need of God's grace. Other people who have this style include Chuck Colson and, in his own unique fashion, Billy Graham. But don't despair. You don't have to start at their level! God can use confrontational Christians at all degrees of development.

If you think this approach is for you, ask the Holy Spirit to guide you to know how, when, and where to direct your words and challenges, as well as the wisdom you'll need to do it with an appropriate mix of grace and truth.

God built diversity into the fabric of His body of believers. And until we realise that, we'll find ourselves needlessly imitating each other's outreach efforts, wastefully duplicating some approaches while harmfully squelching others.

Paul's intellectual approach

Though Paul certainly could confront people with truth when necessary, the hallmark of his approach was his logical and reasoned presentation of the gospel message. Read any of the letters he wrote—Romans is the best example—and you'll see that he was a master at laying out a sound explanation of the central truths about God's nature, our sin, and Christ's solution.

When you look at his background, Paul's organised mind doesn't come as a surprise. He was highly educated, tutored under a man who was reputed to be one of the finest teachers in the land. In his writings, you can see his natural tendency to argue point-counterpoint with imaginary foes who might challenge his positions. Paul was an intellect to be reckoned with.

Can you think of a better person for God to send to the philosophers in Athens? The account is in Acts 17, where you'll find Paul presenting an ingenious argument, starting from the Athenian idol to an unknown god and moving all the way to the only true God and His resurrected Messiah. His approach was so effective that some of his listeners became believers.

It's interesting to note the wisdom God displays in His choice of spokesmen. These philosophers would not have related to Peter's direct, "turn-or-burn!" approach. They needed logic that conclusively proved its point.

And I'll bet there are people in your circle who are just like them. They don't want easy answers or platitudes like, "You'll just have to accept it on faith." To their ears that sounds like, "Leap before you look. Who knows, you might get lucky." They want to know why they should leap at all!

Perhaps you're a Paul. Is the intellectual approach one that fits you? Are you an inquisitive type who enjoys working with ideas and evidence? This style has become more and more important as our society has become increasingly secular. So many seekers need to hear the gospel not only declared but also defined and defended.

This is the style Mark identified with that night several years ago. The pattern he observed in Paul legitimised his own interest in studying philosophy and apologetics (the defence of the Christian faith). Since then he's flourished evangelistically as he's marshalled the evidence supporting Christianity to reach seekers individually and in large groups. And he's built ministries designed to further those efforts. This is also the primary approach used by such well-known Christians as Josh McDowell, D. James Kennedy, and Ravi Zacharias.

The blind man's testimonial approach

Though we know less about him than we do about Peter or Paul, we can be sure about this: the blind man healed by Jesus in John 9 had seen something happen in his life that was worth talking about!

He'd been blind since birth, and regularly sat begging from people passing by. But his routine quickly changed when Jesus came along and gave him the gift of sight. No sooner was he able to see than he was thrust in front of a hostile audience and asked to explain what had happened.

It's interesting that the man refused to enter into theological debate with them (John 9:25), though Paul probably would have been happy to oblige them with a few compelling arguments. And he steered away from confrontation, whereas Peter might have given them a shot of truth. Those responses didn't fit who he was.

Instead, he spoke from his experience and confidently said, "One thing I do know. I was blind but now I see!" That's a difficult declaration to argue with, isn't it? It's pretty hard to escape the implications of such a testimony, even from a fledgling Christian.

Notice that in verse 3 Jesus said this man had been born blind "so that the work of God might be displayed in his life." That's an example of what I've been saying: that we are custom-tailored for a particular approach. God had been preparing this man all of his life for these events and his telling them in a way that would point people toward Christ.

And there are a lot of people who live and work around you who need to hear a similar testimony about how God is working in a believer's life. They might not respond very well to a challenge or an argument, but a personal account of someone's coming to faith would influence them powerfully.

Could that story be yours? Do you, like the man who had been blind, feel comfortable telling others how God led you to Himself? Even if you haven't done that yet, does the idea excite you? Stories like yours can be powerful tools.

Examples of people who effectively use this testimonial approach include Dave Cravecky, the former American baseball pitcher who lost his arm to cancer, and Joni Erickson Tada, a quadriplegic woman whose account of how God helped her through her tragic accident points people clearly toward Him. Another example is Lee Strobel, a former atheist who is now one of our teaching pastors at Willow Creek. He often uses the details of his background to appeal to unbelievers.

Some people are just waiting for a contagious Christian who won't beat around the bush, but who'll clarify the truth of Christ and challenge them to do something about it. Could that Christian be you?

It's important to point out that effective testimonies don't have to be dramatic. Don't exclude yourself from this approach because you have a garden-variety testimony. Maybe you went to church and were religious all your life before you realised that those things didn't make you a Christian. But the story of how you moved from religion into a relationship with Christ will be more relevant to most of your acquaintances than a sensational story of someone coming to Christ out of a life of witchcraft and drugs.

As a matter of fact, the difficulty of personally relating to the dramatic testimony may give your friends an excuse. "People like that *need* religion!" they might say. But your everyday story will relate to their everyday life and show them that they, too, need the grace and leadership of God that you've found.

And if you do have a more dramatic story, ask God to

lead you concerning how much detail to give and to whom to tell it, so that they'll hear the aspects of your experience they can connect with, and be drawn to seek what you've found in Christ.

Matthew's interpersonal approach

By any standard, he was an unlikely candidate. Tax collectors just weren't known for becoming evangelists. Yet that's exactly what happened to Matthew. After accepting Jesus' call to become one of His followers, he decided to do whatever he could to bring along as many of his friends as possible.

So, as we saw in Luke 5:29, he put on a big banquet for all of his tax-collecting buddies in an effort to expose them to Jesus and the new life He offered. Unlike those who utilise the other approaches we've examined, Matthew didn't confront or intellectually challenge them, nor is there any mention of his telling them the story of what had happened to him. Those were simply not his styles.

Rather, he relied on the relationships he'd built with these men over the years and sought to further develop their friendships. He invited them into his home. He spent time with them and ate with them. He did all of this because he genuinely cared about them, and he wanted to influence them toward considering the claims of Christ.

In the preceding chapters, we've talked about the importance of building relationships. As we've seen, the vantage point of friendship gives us the highest possibility of influence in the lives of others. Well, from my experience, those who have the interpersonal style of evangelism *specialise* in this area. They tend to be warm, people-centred individuals who enjoy deep levels of communication and trust with those they're reaching out to.

And many people will never be reached until someone takes the time to build that kind of intimacy with them. Maybe you're an interpersonal evangelist. Do you enjoy having long talks over a cup of coffee with a friend you're trying to reach? Can you patiently listen to another person's concerns without rushing in to tell them what they need to do? Do you enjoy having people into your home, sharing a meal, and spending time in conversation?

A couple of well-known examples of the interpersonal style are Becky Pippert and Joe Aldrich, both of whom have written helpful books on the subject. Churches around the world need a lot more of their members to develop this kind of approach with their own friends and family members as well as the lost people in their wider communities.

The Samaritan woman's invitational approach

Don't you love the way God picks unlikely people to fulfil His divine purposes? We've seen it with the blind man, with Matthew, and now with this woman from Samaria. And, as you get more involved in personal outreach to others, you'll probably feel this way about yourself. I sometimes look at God's activity of touching people through me and say to myself, "Who'd have ever thunk it!" God seems to delight in using ordinary, everyday kinds of people in surprising and exciting ways.

The Samaritan woman had three things going against her: she was a Samaritan, she was a woman, and she was living an immoral lifestyle. Back then, any one of these would be enough to disqualify her from being taken seriously by society. But do you think that stopped Jesus? You can read in John 4 how He ignored all the conventional wisdom and political correctness of the day by striking up a conversation with her.

It didn't take long for the woman to realise that the

man she was talking to was no ordinary Jewish teacher. His prophetic insights and authoritative answers convinced her of His claim to be the Messiah.

So what did she do? She immediately went to her town and brought a bunch of people to the well to hear Jesus for themselves. This simple invitation resulted in His staying in their town for two days. Many of the woman's friends declared, in verse 42, "Now we have heard for ourselves, and we know that this man really is the Saviour of the world."

There are many people who would make great strides in their spiritual journey if someone would go to the effort of strategically inviting them to a seeker-friendly church service or outreach event.

And a lot of non-Christians are open to this approach. A recent poll by researcher George Barna showed, for example, that about twenty-five per cent of the adults in the United States would go to church if a friend would just invite them. Think about it: one in four of your friends would be willing to join you! The primary question you'll need to answer is what kinds of events—church services, concerts, movies, plays, or other programmes in your church or community—would be appropriate to bring them to. Consider their perspective and interests in order to make the best choice.

Although invitations are a great way for all of us to reach out to others, some people, like the woman at the well, have a knack for getting people to go places with them. Maybe you're one of them. Do you find yourself constantly widening the circle of people involved in your activities? Have you found that when there's an outreach event going on your car is getting a bit tight? Maybe it's time to trade it in on a mini-van so you can expand your evangelistic efforts!

It's hard to think of well-known examples of people with the invitational style. Many of these Christians tend to stay out of the limelight. But when you see one you'll probably know it. They love to pick up strays. They're the unsung heroes who make outreach events successful by filling them with people who need to hear the message.

Mark knows someone named Nancy who has this style. A few years back his friends threw a birthday party for him. There were about thirty people there, including one man he'd never seen before. Later, this man took out a violin and played "Happy Birthday". Mark thought it was a nice gesture, but he still wondered who this person was. Finally, someone filled him in. The violinist was trekking across the country alone, and Nancy had met him at the train station. She decided to bring him to Mark's birthday party, just in case he might meet some contagious Christians who'd be able to help him come to Christ. Now *that's* the invitational approach!

I sometimes look at God's activity of touching people through me and say to myself, "Who'd have ever thunk it!" God seems to delight in using ordinary, everyday kinds of people in surprising and exciting ways.

Dorcas's service approach

The Bible says in Acts 9:36 that Dorcas was "always doing good and helping the poor." She was well-known for her loving acts of service which she performed in the name of Christ. Specifically, she made robes and articles of clothing for widows and other needy people in her town.

She was, in effect, a quiet practitioner of what we're

calling the service approach to evangelism. It would have been very hard for people to observe her activity and not get a glimpse of the love of Christ that inspired her. In fact, her work was so important that when she died a premature death, God sent Peter to raise her from the dead and put her back into service.

People who take this approach find it relatively easy to serve others. It's how God made them. They naturally notice needs others don't see, and they find joy in meeting them, even if they don't get a lot of credit for it. Often more quiet types, these people enjoy expressing compassion through tangible forms of action.

Though this style tends to get less press than the others, and it often takes a much longer period of time before producing spiritual results, it's one of the most important of all the evangelistic approaches. That's because service-style evangelists touch people nobody else can reach.

Ginger, a woman at our church, had a brother with whom she was trying to share Christ. But he was into New Age ideas and was disinterested in Christianity. So she did what came naturally to her and her confrontational style—she challenged him with the claims of Christ. When that didn't seem to make a dent, she studied and came to him with reasons why he should change his position. She tried everything she could think of, but nothing got through. Finally, all hope seemed to dissipate when he moved his wife and kids away to join a New Age religious sect.

But God had another card up His sleeve. When Ginger's brother moved into his new home, he soon met the people who lived next-door. They turned out to be wonderful neighbours. These people were constantly doing things for him, like helping him get settled in, lending a hand when something needed to be fixed, bringing over food when someone in his family was sick. Just ordinary acts of service—done out of their love for Christ.

These people brought down the wall between Ginger's brother and God, brick by brick. And within a year's time, he had committed his life to Christ, moved his family back home, and celebrated his first communion sitting next to Ginger at one of our worship services!

Can you see why this style needs to be celebrated? Those neighbours will probably never be famous, but God is using their efforts to reach those the rest of us haven't got a clue how to reach.

You may not have the knowledge of Paul or the courage of Peter and the Samaritan woman. But you're a whiz at making meals or fixing cars. I hope you can see how those things, and so many others like them, can be done in a way that points people to God.

Being yourself

I hope you've been encouraged as you've read about these different approaches to spreading the faith. Maybe you've breathed a sigh of relief as you've realised that you can be yourself, and that God knew what He was doing when He made you.

Let me emphasise that nobody fits perfectly into just one of these styles. In fact, you'll probably find opportunities to use all of them. The point is that God designed diversity on His team; and each member is stronger in some styles than in others. You might come up with style number seven or eight, and that's fine, too.

The important thing to know is that the most contagious Christians are those who've learned to work within the design God has given them. They identify approaches that work for them, and then they develop and deploy them to advance the Kingdom. They also team up with other Christians who have different styles, so that their combined strengths can be used to reach virtually any kind of seeker.

In this section we've talked about the need to get closer to those we hope to reach, and offered some practical ways to do so. We've also looked at various approaches that will help you be authentic and natural in the process. The next big issue is content. What do you actually *say* to the person about God? Read on, as we look at ways to raise spiritual topics of conversation.

SECTION FOUR

The Power of Clear Communication

HP + CP + *CC* = MI

CHAPTER TEN

Starting Spiritual Conversations

"Whose cab is this anyway? And why are *you* driving it?"

I couldn't help asking that question after noticing that the face of the driver at the wheel didn't match the picture on the taxi's dashboard.

It was Christmas eve, I was with my family in a southern U.S. city, and we were in this taxi with who-knows-who driving us to our hotel—or so we hoped.

"Oh, it belongs to a friend of mine," he replied. I thought, *Yeah, that's what they all say.* So I decided to check him out further. I tapped on the time meter and said, "Are you sure this thing is working right?"

"As a matter of fact," he said, "It's ten per cent off." Trying my luck, I said, "Well, it's Christmas time—I'll bet it's reading to my advantage, right?"

"Oh, no," he shot back. "You'll have to pay me ten per cent more than what it's reading."

I was amazed at the nerve this man had. First he was illegally driving someone else's taxi, and now he was trying to con me! After talking with him a little more, I came to the conclusion that my initial impressions were correct: it was going to take a strong, unorthodox approach to get through to a person like this.

Having noticed his foreign accent, I said to him, "I'm curious. What part of the world are you from?" He responded by naming his home country, which was in the Middle East. So I said to him, "Based on where you're from, I'm guessing that you're a Muslim. Am I right?"

"Yes, as a matter of fact, you are," he said, perking up a bit.

I continued, "So, are you a devout Muslim? Is your faith something you take seriously? I mean, do you plan on going to Paradise when you die?" He sputtered and coughed a little, and didn't seem to know quite what to say, so I went on.

"You see, I'm a serious Christian, and I've always wondered something that, well, maybe you could explain to me: Why do you follow the teachings of a dead guy?"

About then he almost swerved off the road. It seemed pretty clear that I had gotten his full attention!

"Huh?" he said. "What do you mean?"

"Well," I said, "I know you worship Allah, and you believe that Muhammad is Allah's spokesman. But he's dead. In fact, we could fly over there right now and see his grave—so why would you follow a dead guy?"

He seemed to be scrambling for words, so I added, "You know, the Bible teaches very clearly that Jesus Christ rose from the dead. My family and I follow someone who is actually alive today."

"Does the Bible really say that Jesus rose from the dead?" he asked. "I tried to read a Bible once, and I didn't see that in there."

How you raise topics of faith will depend on your personality, the subject matter you tend to talk to people about, and your own particular style of evangelism.

"Well, somebody probably gave you one with some pages missing," I said. "I could get you one that has all the pages, and you could read it for yourself. Trust me; it's in there. Jesus is resurrected, Muhammad is dead and, in my opinion, you really ought to think this over!"

When we arrived at our hotel, I was glad we had a few more minutes to talk. I assured him that my purpose was not to question the sincerity of his faith or, for that matter, the idea that Muhammad genuinely believed in what he taught.

But before we parted, I challenged him with the fact that we couldn't both be right. "Five seconds after each of us dies, we're both going to find out who believed the truth," I told him, "And I'm betting my eternity on the One who came back from the dead."

Can you understand why my wife cringes when I start talking to people about these topics? How a sweet, soft-spoken introvert like Lynne ended up marrying someone like me, I'll never know!

Later in the hotel my teenage daughter, Shauna, said to me, "So what was *that*? Is that what you call *evangelism*?"

It was a question you might be asking as well!

But don't miss the point: Regardless of our individual styles, we've all got to be alert, looking for opportunities to talk to people about Christ. And sometimes that will require taking risks, along with the willingness to be creative in how we raise such critically important topics of conversation. The way I did it in that situation was not the only way to do it, and it may not have been the best way, either.

But it was a way that fit me and, as I explained later that evening to Shauna, it was one that seemed appropriate for that taxi driver, given his character and personality. I just don't think anything other than a strong, straightforward approach would have caught his attention. And who knows, maybe it was used by God to turn this man into a serious truth seeker, one who will end up eventually following Christ. Wouldn't *that* be exciting news?

Putting it into words

As we begin this next section, let me remind you of something we discussed earlier: It's not enough to merely have high potency and close proximity; we've got to get to the next step in the formula if we want to maximise our spiritual impact on others. That step is CC, which stands for *clear communication*. We've got to *talk* about our faith, putting spiritual concepts into plain everyday words.

The apostle Paul was adamant about this in Romans 10, where he warned that people won't figure out the message on their own. Even closely watching the life of a contagious Christian won't be enough. Somebody has to articulate the gospel to them by spelling out who God is, what kind of damage our sin has caused, and how each of us needs to receive the forgiveness and life that Christ offers.

But in order for that to happen, we must take the initiative and steer discussions toward spiritual topics. That's where things really get exciting. And it's what this chapter is all about.

Before we go into detail on ways we can start spiritual conversations, I want to caution you about two things. First, only a limited number of the examples I'm about to describe will actually fit you. How you raise topics of faith will depend on your personality, the subject matter you tend to talk to people about, and your own particular style of evangelism.

For example, my approach with the cab driver was

natural for me, because I lean toward the confrontational style of evangelism. It is relatively easy for me to get into deeper levels of conversation with strangers, although my talk with the driver likely would have had more impact if I'd had some time to start building a real friendship first.

So as I present various illustrations of how you can begin spiritual conversations, take special note of any you think you could actually use, and write down any other ones that occur to you while you're reading. My primary goal is to stimulate your thinking so that you'll find approaches that uniquely fit you.

Second, before you'll be able to initiate these kinds of discussions, you must start with the heart-felt assurance that not only is your life better now than it was before you knew God, but the lives of others will be better, too, even through the tough times. Without this assurance, it's almost impossible to motivate yourself to take any meaningful action. You'll also need a desire to spread His message that's strong enough to move you to pray regularly for opportunities and then to watch for them throughout each day.

My assumption is that you've read this far because these prequalifiers are largely in place. If, however, you sense a need for a firmer foundation, I'd suggest these activities. Begin by listing some of the benefits of knowing Christ. Then review the promises God makes to us in the Bible for this life and the next. Finally, thank and worship Him for the countless benefits of knowing Him. After doing these things for a while, you'll wonder how *anyone* could pass up His offer of forgiveness and divine guidance!

Let's look at three methods for how you can steer discussions toward spiritual subjects. We'll call them the direct method, the indirect method, and the invitational method.

The direct method

This approach to redirecting conversations does just what it says. It doesn't wait for opportunities to avail themselves; it *creates* them. The way it works is simple. You straightforwardly raise a spiritual topic and then see if the person is interested in talking about it. While you don't force anyone to discuss matters of faith, you do open wide the doorway to doing so.

This is the approach I used with the taxi driver when I asked him if he was a serious Muslim. Here is another opener I've often found very helpful, probably because it makes people curious: *"If you'd ever like to know the difference between religion and Christianity, let me know. I'd be happy to talk to you about it."*

This is a modern-day equivalent of what Jesus did in John 4. He piqued the interest of the woman at the well by telling her He could give her living water. She'd never heard of it, but it intrigued her.

Before you'll be able to initiate these kinds of discussions, you must start with the heart-felt assurance that not only is your life better now than it was before you knew God, but the lives of others will be better, too, even through the tough times.

I've used this approach while jogging at the health club. I've run up next to individuals I've got to know, said it to them, and then run on ahead. They may ignore it, bring it up later, or catch up to me and ask for an explanation. I'm not pressuring them or forcing it upon them. I'm merely checking to see if they're interested.

Sometimes people come back to me and say, "What was that you were saying to me about religion and Christianity? I thought Christianity *was* a religion." And then I've responded by explaining the central difference that sets our faith apart from other religious systems, using the "Do vs. Done" illustration that I'll detail in the next chapter.

Another fairly direct phrase I've found helpful over the years begins by asking the customary question, "How's it going today?" The person will reflexively say, "Oh, fine," whether things are going great or their life is falling apart. Then I try to discern whether the person seems at all open, and I pray quickly to see how the Holy Spirit might be leading. If all the lights look green, I'll look the person in the eye and say, "Ahh, come on, you can tell *me*. How's it *really* going?"

I'm rarely disappointed with their response. Most of the time they start by testing my sincerity: "Are you sure you want to know?" And when I tell them I am, they'll say, "Man, thanks for asking..." and they begin to open up. By the end of the conversation, I've almost always found it natural to assure them not only that I care, but that God cares, too, and that I'd enjoy telling them more about Him whenever they're ready.

Briefly, here are a few other direct conversation starters:

- "I'm curious, do you ever think about spiritual matters?"
- "Who, in your opinion, was Jesus Christ?"
- "What's your spiritual background? Were you taught a particular religious perspective as you grew up?"
- "Do you ever wonder what happens to us when we die?"
- "What do you think a real Christian is?"
- "Where are you heading in your spiritual journey?"

What continually amazes me is how such simple lines can begin a process that ultimately revolutionises the life of the other person. Don't let the simplicity of these questions cause you to discount their usefulness. They can literally open doorways into eternity.

Those in the marketplace commonly ask each other, "How's your year going?" But rather than give a standard reply, why not answer with something like this: "Well, financially, okay; family-wise, pretty well; and spiritually, things are great. Which one do you want to talk about?"

The indirect method

A few years ago, Mark and Heidi were standing in line outside a well-known restaurant. It was a long wait and, being extroverts, they managed to meet most of the people near them. The man right in front of them was particularly interesting. He was in charge of running the lights for a major network television programme. Deciding to take a risk, Mark transitioned the conversation by saying, "You know, since you're a lighting expert, maybe you can explain something to me about some lights we used for a special concert at our church."

As he'd anticipated, Mark didn't see a great degree of interest in the man's eyes, at least so far. But he went on: "You see, we rented these automated lights that are mounted on the stage and move around by themselves, and they project various colours, and sometimes they have laser or strobe effects."

Now the guy's eyes were getting big. "Those are

called Vari-Lites, and they're computer-controlled by highly trained technicians. I've never even run them before.... Did you say you had one of those in a *church*?"

Matter-of-factly, Mark replied, "No, we had about thirty of them. They were mounted on motorised set pieces that came down from the ceiling during the programme. It was pretty interesting to watch."

By now, this man was fascinated. "That's incredible! What kind of a church do you go to, anyway?"

Mark was wondering if he'd ever ask! He replied, "It's a church that takes a very modern approach to representing a very old message, which is simply this—" and he went on to briefly explain the gospel.

Before they parted, this man gave Mark his business card so he could mail him a videotape of the programme he'd described. And it all started with a simple comment about some lights in a church!

As this example illustrates, the indirect method takes some element of the discussion topic and utilises it to turn the conversation toward matters of God, the church, or faith. There's almost no limit to the ways this can be done. With a little planning and practice, almost anyone can master this approach. Here are a few other illustrations:

Business

Those in the marketplace commonly ask each other, "How's your year going?" But rather than give a standard reply, why not answer with something like this: "Well, financially, okay; family-wise, pretty well; and spiritually, things are great. Which one do you want to talk about?"

They may be ready to talk on a deeper level, or they may respond by saying, "Well, let's go back to the financial part. . . .” That’s okay; at least you’ve planted some seeds for future conversations.

Relocations

When acquaintances have recently moved to a new neighbourhood, it’s natural to ask questions about whether they’ve found good places to shop, dine out, or get their car repaired. Why not add a query concerning whether they’ve found a good church? Even if they tell you that they weren’t looking, it’s a natural lead-in to talking about faith-related topics.

An especially creative example comes from Jim, an attorney I know who recently moved his law practice to a new location. Since then he’s been telling people, “It’s great. The office is now only twenty minutes from my house—and just five minutes from the church.” Even if out of mere politeness, people often respond by asking him about his church involvements.

Hobbies and spare time

When you’re talking to someone about your hobbies or what you do in your spare time, it’s easy to include some ministry-related activity that you enjoy. For instance, if you work with the sound system at your church, you could say, “Well, on weekends I like mountain biking and working with sound equipment.” The automatic response of many people will be to ask for details. Similar approaches could be used in almost any area, whether you work with lighting, construction, decorating, cooking, cleaning, music, teaching, or ushering.

Perhaps you help with the children’s programme. When talking with friends about their children, it’s easy to say something like, “I’ve found that children can really be a challenge. What really keeps me on my toes is watching forty of them each weekend.” After they pick their jaw up off the floor, you can explain that you’re part of a teaching team at the church and mention, "by the way, you should see some of the exciting programmes we're doing with the children."

With a little creativity, any ministry role can be described in interesting terms that will create curiosity. And it's a short step to move from talking about your church involvement to the love of God that drives it.

Nature

What about using the wonders of creation to point to the Creator? If you're with some friends at the zoo, it's a simple matter to look at a giraffe and say, "You know, God must have been *laughing* when He made that one. What a great sense of humour He must have!"

Mark used a similar approach once when he was backpacking in the Rocky Mountains and befriended a man who was camping alone. While hiking together, they noticed the amazing variety of wildflowers along the trail. Mark finally said, "What an imagination God must have, to make so many different shapes and colours of flowers." It was just a simple, benign observation—one that could be agreed with, argued about, or ignored. His friend's response was, "I guess that would make sense if you believed in God, but I don't."

A response like this does *not* spell failure. Remember that the goal is to raise the topic, not to evoke an affirming response. In fact, this situation very much met the objective, because in saying he didn't believe in God, this man had blown the conversation wide open. Remember that Mark prefers the intellectual style of evangelism, so he *salivates* at the opportunity to talk to an atheist about God!

It was natural for him to say back, "Oh, that's interesting. Why don't you believe in God?" And that brief exchange turned into a conversation that lasted the rest of the afternoon and into the evening—until the campfire died out.

Music

Maybe you follow the music charts, and you know a lot of the popular songs and performers. That knowledge can easily be utilised to draw attention to contemporary Christian musicians or secular artists who've trusted Christ. Amy Grant, BeBe and CeCe Winans, and Michael W. Smith are Christian artists who are known and respected in the music industry. Secular musicians who are open about their faith include Kerry Livgren from the group Kansas, Mark Farner from Grand Funk, Philip Bailey from Earth, Wind & Fire, country singer Ricky Skaggs, '60s hit-maker Dion DiMucci, and Canadian rocker Bruce Cockburn.

With a little creativity, any ministry role can be described in interesting terms that will create curiosity. And it's a short step to move from talking about your church involvement to the love of God that drives it.

Another angle is to talk about the message in the lyrics of a popular song that raises spiritual issues, even if it might have been written or performed by a non-Christian. Examples from the past include "Show Me the Way", by Dennis DeYoung of the group Styx, "Kyrie", by Mister Mister, and "Something to Believe In", by Poison. These can lead into talking about the answers you've found to the important questions they raise.

Sports

This category is similar to the last one, and it has ever-increasing possibilities because so many well-known athletes are becoming Christians. In recent years numerous biographies, articles, and television programmes have described this exciting turn of events. In fact, there's now a magazine dedicated to featuring Christian athletes called *Sports Spectrum*.

Well-known examples in the USA include football players Mike Singletary, Dennis Byrd, Warren Moon, and Jeff Hostetler; baseball players Joe Carter, Orel Hershiser, and Dave Dravecky; basketball players Mark Price, A. C. Greene, and David Robinson; tennis player Michael Chang; golfers Betsy King and Paul Azinger; track and field medalists Madeline Mims and Evelyn Ashford; and Olympic decathlete Dave Johnson (of "Dan and Dave" television commercial fame).

For Christians who follow sports, it's pretty easy to refer to a recent game or event and tell friends about a particular athlete on the team who's a believer. This will often expand into a wider discussion about what that means. The opportunity can then be furthered by giving them a copy of a book, article, or tape about that athlete, or even an invitation to an outreach event where that person will be telling his or her story.

Shared struggles

When you find you have areas of difficulty in common with someone, it's the most natural thing in the world to tell that person how you've been helped by wisdom from the Bible, caring Christian friends, or divine intervention. Believers who are in Twelve-Step programmes have used this approach for years: "Can I tell you about the higher power who has changed my life?"

This method can be effective, whether it's a major crisis or a relatively minor problem. It might be a lack of communication in your marriage, questions about disciplining your children, or a need for learning to manage food, time, or finances.

You don't have to have the problem solved. You just need to have found practical help and made some progress. That's enough to warrant turning discussions from the source of the frustration to spiritual solutions that have made a difference for you. For example, "My wife and I have had similar frustrations in our communication patterns. Can I tell you about some biblical principles I've learned that have really had an impact on our marriage?" Or, "I know what you mean about feeling like giving up on your adolescent, but I'd like to show you a book by a Christian counsellor whose advice really helped my husband and I get through that era with our children."

It's been said that misery loves company. I think that's all the more true when that company can point to a source of supernatural assistance.

Holidays

I've noticed throughout my years in ministry that people are often more open to God during the holiday seasons of Christmas and Easter. These holidays provide excellent opportunities to turn conversations toward the spiritual side: "So what about the baby in the manger—do you buy into the idea that He was God's Son?" Or, "It's pretty clear Jesus was no ordinary baby. Why do you think God would go to all the effort of sending His Son to earth?"

At Easter you might ask, "Do you think the Easter celebration is based on fact or fiction?" Or, if you know the person is sceptical about the resurrection, you could ask, "So what do you think happened to Jesus' body—it clearly wasn't in the tomb by Sunday morning?"

When you find you have areas of difficulty in common with someone, it's the most natural thing in the world to tell that person how you've been helped by wisdom from the Bible, caring Christian friends, or divine intervention.

If you know your friends have a church background, you could ask about any memories the holidays evoke. Similar approaches include asking if they think there's really anything good about Good Friday, or what they're thankful for at Harvest supper, or which kinds of freedom mean the most to them on Remembrance Sunday. You might also have a conversation about holiday traditions their families keep, and what those traditions mean to them. These can turn into opportunities to invite your friends to a holiday event at your church or in your community.

Are you getting the idea that we could go on and on listing ideas for many more areas? Good. That means we probably don't need to do so. But you do. You'll need to take the topics you frequently talk with people about and, like the examples above, figure out creative ways to ease into conversations related to your faith.

The invitational method

Inviting friends to seeker-oriented outreach events not only encourages them to attend; it can also raise spiritual topics of discussion. Since we know people will often decline, why not just plan for that possibility and be prepared to make the most of it? Graciously accept their decision, but then ask them to tell you about their own spiritual heritage.

Here's an example of how you might respond in that kind of situation: "That's fine, Bob, I know you've got a lot going on right now. There'll be another chance to do something like this together. But you know, I am curious about your spiritual background. Were you raised with any particular religious point of view?" If you make it open-ended and relaxed enough, people will feel free to let you know their perspective—positive or negative—and that can be a great discussion starter.

While we're on the topic of inviting people to events, let me offer a few tips that will increase your chances of success. First, be very careful to select events—whether concerts, plays, movies, church services, or social gatherings—that you're confident will be done with excellence and with sensitivity toward outsiders. Unfortunately, many well-meaning outreach programmes do more damage than good.

Second, put something in their hands that will give details about the events. It can be a printed brochure or handwritten memo, but it's important that they have a visual reminder to help them show up at the right time and place.

Third, offer them a lift. Suggest having a meal or coffee together after the event. These extra touches will show friendship and provide a good context for talking about what you've just seen and heard.

Overriding principles

Whatever method you use for starting a spiritual conversation, keep in mind these pointers:

Pray hard

There's no substitute for consistent prayer. Ask God not only to give you wisdom and to guide your words, but also to help others be open and interested.

Talk to people individually

Peer pressure isn't just an adolescent phenomenon. I've found it's always easier to talk to people one-on-one so that they won't be embarrassed or concerned about the opinions of anyone who's listening.

Pique curiosity

Don't feel like you always have to bring up your faith in a direct fashion. Drop hints and create curiosity the way Jesus did when He mentioned living water to the woman at the well. Let them further the conversation by asking you what you're referring to.

Rely on reciprocal reflexes

That's a fancy way of saying that if you want to tell someone about your own interests or beliefs, start by asking them about theirs. They'll naturally answer your questions and then ask you a similar one.

Seize split-second opportunities

Each day we have conversations with people that provide us with the chance to raise topics of faith, but most of us aren't prepared for them. When others ask us how we're doing, most of us give a standard, safe response.

We've got to be willing to go out on a limb and say the unexpected. It's one thing to see the split-second opportunity but quite another to seize it. I don't know of any way around it—it's going to take some courage to get the ball rolling and actually initiate spiritual conversations. Christianity that's really contagious takes some guts.

So next time somebody asks you what you've got going on during the weekend or what you're planning to do next summer, you've got a choice to make. Do you abort the adventure before it starts by merely talking about weeding the garden or visiting the relatives in

Scotland? Or will you take a deep breath and give God a chance to really use you as you describe the critically important topic you're learning about at church, or the exciting weekend you're planning with the kids in the youth group?

I don't know of any way around it—it's going to take some courage to get the ball rolling and actually initiate spiritual conversations. Christianity that's really contagious takes some guts.

There are two doors you can go through. One is safe, familiar, and uneventful. The other is risky, uncharted, and full of spiritual potential. Which door will you choose?

Don't underestimate their degree of interest

Most of us routinely make the mistake of assuming people aren't really that interested in spiritual truth. But many people today are getting tired of living without ultimate purpose: putting in hours at the office, paying the bills and making ends meet, keeping themselves entertained with things that rust, fade, and wear out. More and more of them are coming to the point of saying, "There's got to be more to life than *this*!" In fact, many of them are actively searching for answers, though often in all the wrong places. That's why religious sects and cults are growing so fast.

And here we are, holding the keys to meaning in this life and hope for the next. We've got to rub shoulders with those who so desperately need what we have. Then we need to start some spiritual conversations, and find out who's interested.

When you begin this process, I predict you're going to be surprised by how many people are not only open, but genuinely interested. I know, because I'm constantly surprised myself.

One more thing: You might be wondering about what to actually *tell* people once the conversation is started. Good question! That's the subject of our next chapter, which is probably the most important one in the book.

CHAPTER ELEVEN

Making the Message Clear

The moment is indelibly etched in my memory.

Lynne and I were on a sailing trip. After anchoring in a harbour for the night, we got into a conversation with some people who invited us to come to their boat later to spend time socialising with them and a few of their friends.

We accepted their invitation, and that evening we got into our dinghy and motored over to their yacht. They were a very hospitable group of people, and we enjoyed getting to know them. It soon became clear that they weren't believers. But when in the course of our discussions they asked what I did for a living, none of them seemed taken aback by the fact that I was a pastor of a church. They were just cordial and friendly, and we had a good time.

It was when we were in the process of leaving that the moment came. Lynne had already climbed down the ladder into the dinghy and I was halfway down myself when one of the people who had invited us aboard said, "Say, Bill, before you leave can you answer a question? I've always wanted to ask a Christian what it means to become one. Could you tell all of us?"

There I was, one foot in the dinghy and one hand on their boat's railing, looking up at all of these people who were standing their holding their piña coladas, and waiting to see what I'd say. I knew I had their undivided attention—for about forty-five seconds—to summarise what it means to become a real Christian.

Putting on my shoes

Let's do a freeze frame so I can ask you a question: If you'd been in my place, how would *you* have responded? Would you have been ready to give a clear and succinct response to such an important question?

If your answer is no, you're not alone. Whether you're a brand new believer or a veteran follower of Christ, this kind of situation puts you to the test. What often happens is your mind goes blank, or you find yourself stumbling around trying to figure out where to start, and all the while you feel the pressure of heaven and hell hanging in the balance.

We're helpless to initiate any action that can change our situation. I sometimes describe it as being "morally bankrupt", with nothing in our account with which to pay off our debts. Thankfully, the story doesn't end there.

Yet the Bible warns us to "always be prepared to give an answer to everyone who asks you to give the reason for the hope that you have" (1 Peter 3:15). Elsewhere we're told that we should "be prepared in season and out of season" (2 Timothy 4:2). And Jesus called us "the light of the world." As we saw earlier, that entails not only living as shining examples for Christ, but also lucidly expressing His message so others can see the truth of the gospel.

I think it's high time a lot more of us take these commands seriously. These are not merely suggestions, they are divine imperatives, delivered by God for the sake of lost people who matter deeply to Him. And the degree to which we heed them has a direct bearing on the eternal outcome of people all around us.

What these people actually *do* with the message is between them and God. But it's our responsibility to make it as clear to them as possible. So let me commend you for your effort not only to read but also to apply the content in this chapter. I'm going to spell out what the gospel is and then provide some ideas on how we can convey it to others.

Four points to ponder

The goal of this chapter is twofold: First, I want to make certain we understand the gospel message for ourselves. Second, I want to be sure we know how to illustrate it for those we talk to.

So let's start with ourselves. We're going to look briefly at four primary points we need to know in order to get a firm grasp of the gospel. They are God, us, Christ, and you. After examining these, we'll discuss ways we can clearly and concisely communicate the message to others.

God

There are many aspects of God's nature that we could study, but He has three characteristics that are especially relevant in evangelism. The first one is that He is *loving*. Out of His compassion He made us and desires to have a relationship with us. Even though we're sinners who have rebelled against Him, He continues to patiently extend His love to us.

Many people prefer to stop right here, but there's more that needs to be said. You see, God is also *holy*. This means that He is absolutely pure, and He is separate from everything that is impure.

This was driven home to me one day after we'd built our main auditorium at Willow Creek, and the time came for final inspection. Before the construction company representatives arrived, one of our staff members set up a spotlight and shone it into the dark areas of the ceiling, above the catwalks. A number of previously obscured imperfections became glaringly visible.

Then the construction people showed up. As soon as they saw the spotlight, they told us firmly that we couldn't examine the building in that way. They even pulled out our contract, which specified that the final inspection was to be done under normal room lighting.

That incident has always reminded me of God's holiness and its affect on us. Under normal lighting, our lives tend to look pretty good, with no serious moral flaws or blemishes. But then God comes and shines the brilliant light of His holiness on our actions, thoughts, and intentions, and what shows up is not pretty.

That leads us to a third characteristic of God: He is *just*. In other words, He's like a good judge who can't wink at a broken law: Rather, He must mete out justice.

A few years ago in Scotland, a man murdered a member of his family. But by the time he was brought to trial, the judge decided he'd already punished himself enough, and he let him go. It doesn't take a lot of imagination to guess how the public responded: "What? That's not fair: We want justice! Get that judge out of there, and replace him with a good one who'll uphold the law."

Well, God is a perfect judge who will dispense justice to everyone fairly.

When God first created us, He made us good, without sin. But we abused our freedom, rebelled against Him, and become evil.

Furthermore, as we've just seen, God's holiness exposes us for what we are and His justice deals fairly with the sin we've committed. Unfortunately, the seriousness of our sin requires God to pronounce upon us the death penalty. This means both physical death and spiritual death, which is separation from God in a place called hell.

And to cap off the bad news, we're helpless to initiate any action that can change our situation. I sometimes describe it as being "morally bankrupt", with nothing in our account with which to pay off our debts. Thankfully, the story doesn't end there.

Christ

Jesus Christ was uniquely able to solve our dilemma because He was both God and man. As God, He had the power and authority to devise a plan for our salvation. As a man, He was able to execute the plan by taking upon Himself the punishment we deserved.

The central truth of the gospel is that Christ died in our place, as our substitute. He suffered the death penalty debt for us. In so doing, He expressed the love of God, upheld the holiness of God, and satisfied the justice of God.

He did all of that so that He could turn around and offer us His forgiveness, friendship, and leadership as a gift. We don't deserve it, we didn't pay for it, and we can't earn it. The only way we can receive it is to humbly bow before Him, admit our waywardness, and say yes to His incredible offer.

When we do that, our sin-debt is paid in full, and we receive the promise of eternal life in heaven. We also gain the ongoing companionship of the gift-giver Himself, who will be there to lead us, guide us, and lovingly bring us correction when we need it.

I like the way it's summed up in a praise song we sing at our worship services:

> He paid a debt He did not owe
> I owed a debt I could not pay
> I needed someone to wash my sins away
> And now I sing a brand new song
> Amazing Grace, all day long
> Christ Jesus paid the debt
> That I could never pay
>
> (Author Unknown)

Before we go on to the last of our four points, let's look at a couple of questions people often raise about the role Christ played in gaining our salvation. First, some people ask why any price had to be paid at all. "Why couldn't God just forgive and forget, as we can?"

But suppose you had a brand new car parked in front of your home, and a neighbour accidentally ran into it. Though you can forgive him and release him from any responsibility, you'll still have a problem: Who's going to pay for the dent? Since you let him off the hook, you're going to be left having to pay for the repairs yourself.

It's perplexing to me that in spite of the Bible's emphasis that we must individually receive Christ and His gift of salvation, this is the most overlooked part of the message in a lot of churches today.

Similarly, we've done damage by sinning against God. And He, too, was willing to forgive us and restore our relationship with Him. It's ours for the asking. But He still had to pay for the damage. He was left holding the bill—the death penalty—which He paid by coming as one of us and dying on the cross in our place (Acts 20:28).

The second question some people ask is why *Christ* had to pay that penalty: "What kind of justice is there in having Jesus, an innocent bystander, suffer instead of me?" Some people have even compared this to the old "whipping boy" practice, a horribly unjust system of substitute punishment used in mediaeval times. When a young member of a royal family broke the rules, the child's teachers did not dare discipline him directly. Instead, they would whip a slave boy in front of the offender. This was supposed to make the child feel bad enough to reform and stay in line. Of course, it was grossly unfair and in no way served justice.

How is this different from what Christ did? The answer lies in His identity. He's not some reluctant bystander who God forced onto the scene as a whipping boy to take our punishment. *He is actually the God we have sinned against.*

Philippians 2:6–8 spells this out when it says that Christ was "in very nature God," but that He was willing to let go temporarily of His lofty position for us. It says He "made himself nothing, taking the very nature of a servant, being made in human likeness. And being found in appearance as a man, he humbled himself and became obedient to death—even death on a cross!"

And He says to us, "I love you, I've willingly paid the penalty you owed, and I want to forgive you. Would you trust and follow Me?"

You

The ball is now in your court, and it's up to you to decide what you're going to do with it. Jesus paid the price of salvation for the whole world, but only those who say yes to Him will actually receive His forgiveness.

People enjoy hearing other people's stories. A concise and well-thought-out description of your own journey to faith can have a powerful effect on your listeners. It's hard to argue with.

It's perplexing to me that in spite of the Bible's emphasis that we must individually receive Christ and His gift of salvation, this is the most overlooked part of the message in a lot of churches today. Many people are left with the impression that if they go to church, or are born into a Christian family, or try to be moral and religious, then they are automatically made right with God. But it's not true. Anyone who relies on their personal efforts to get into God's family is eventually going to experience the world's worst nightmare. Listen to the warning Jesus gave in Matthew 7:21–23: "Not everyone who says to me, 'Lord, Lord,' will enter the kingdom of heaven, but only he who does the will of my Father who is in heaven. Many will say to me on that day, 'Lord, Lord, did we not prophesy in your name, and in your name drive out demons and perform many miracles?' Then I will tell them plainly, 'I never knew you. Away from me, you evildoers!' "

So for the sake of those who need to be reached, we've got to be crystal clear about the fact that a personal response is essential. Each of us has to receive the forgiveness and leadership of Christ individually. And when we do, the Bible assures us that the Holy Spirit will immediately take residence within us and begin to change us from the inside out.

We can't make that decision for others and we shouldn't push them to make it prematurely. But we've got to be sure they understand that there is no other way. Furthermore, we need to be prepared to help them take that step across the line of faith, a subject we'll talk about in chapter thirteen.

I hope that by going over these four points—God, us, Christ, and you—you've been able to improve your mastery of the basic elements of the gospel message. Now we're going to shift to the second objective of this chapter, which is to give you some practical tools you can use to communicate this message to others.

Illustrations for making the message clear

The following illustrations present the four points of the gospel using terms and pictures that will help your listener understand and remember it. I'm presenting several different ones so you'll have options to choose from, based on your circumstances and the person you're talking to. Give special attention to any that you think would relate well to the people on your Impact List.

Do vs. Done

This is the most simple and succinct tool I know for telling others about Christ. It gets right to the heart of the issue so many people are confused about. That is, it addresses the question of what part our own efforts play in attaining God's salvation.

Since this illustration is verbal, without need for any props or visual aids, it's a good one to use in ordinary conversations, including talks on the telephone.

It's also great for times when you know you've got to say it cleanly and quickly—like when you're on a ladder, halfway between a sailboat and a dinghy, looking up at a handful of slightly inebriated seekers! That's what I tried to do on that occasion.

"Well, first you've got to realise the difference

between religion and Christianity," I started. "Religion is spelled 'D-O', because it consists of the things people *do* to try to somehow gain God's forgiveness and favour.

"But the problem is that you never know when you've done enough. It's like being a salesman who knows he must meet a quota but never being told what it is. You can never be sure that you've actually done enough. Worse yet, the Bible tells us in Romans 3:23 that we *never* can do enough. We'll always fall short of God's perfect standard.

"But thankfully," I went on, "Christianity is spelled differently. It's spelled 'D-O-N-E', which means that what we could never do for ourselves, Christ has already done for us. He lived the perfect life we could never live, and He willingly died on the cross to pay the penalty we owed for the wrongs we've done.

"To become a real Christian is to humbly receive God's gift of forgiveness and to commit to following His leadership. When we do that, He adopts us into His family, and begins to change us from the inside out."

I was glad to have such a concise tool as the "Do vs. Done" illustration. Let me encourage you to master it as well. It's easy to learn, yet it's very effective as a tool to help people understand the central tenets of the Christian faith, especially those who think they can get to heaven by being good enough.

*The Bridge Illustration**

This is probably the best-known and most frequently used gospel illustration around, and for good reason. It graphically shows people their predicament and God's solution.

---

* Adapted from *The Bridge*, © 1981 by the Navigators. Used by permission of NavPress. All rights reserved.

Many gospel tracts and booklets are built around this illustration. You may find one of them to be helpful for explaining the gospel, though I prefer to make it more personal by drawing it out on a piece of paper. Even if you decide to use a printed version, I'd still suggest that you learn how to draw it so you can be prepared to use the illustration at any time. Also, be aware that some people could feel put off if you pull out a piece of preprinted literature.

After you've got a spiritual conversation started, you can casually tell the person that you've learned a helpful diagram for understanding the central message of the Bible, and then ask if they'd like to see it. You'll find, as I have, that many people will be genuinely interested.

I usually start by saying "We matter to God. He made us, and He wants to have a relationship with us," and I write "Us" on one side of a napkin, placemat, or whatever piece of paper is readily available, and "God" on the other:

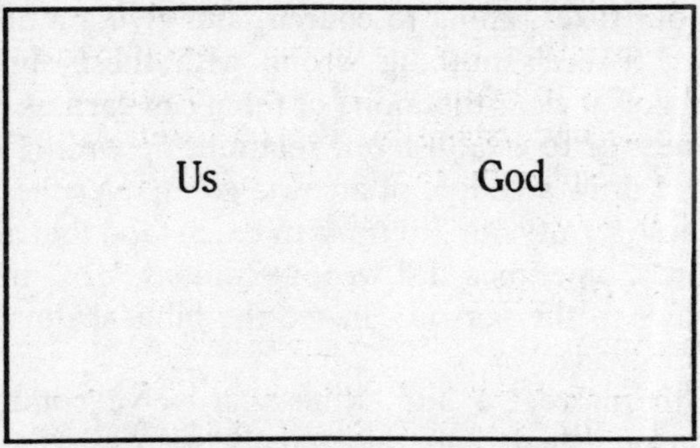

Then I explain the problem. "We rebelled against God. Both actively and passively, we've all disobeyed Him. And our sins have separated us from Him, and broken off the relationship." And I draw lines by both words in such a way that they form walls around a great chasm, separating us from God:

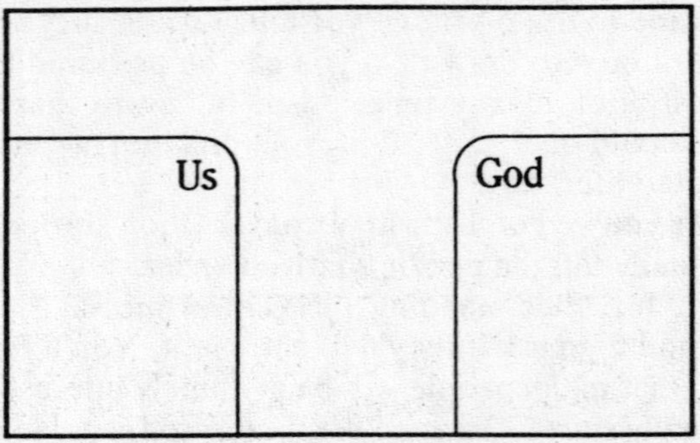

"To varying degrees, most of us are aware of our distance from God," I continue. "I know I was, and you may be, too. And so we start doing all kinds of things to try to get back to Him, like being a helpful neighbour, paying our taxes, going to church, and giving money to charities. There's nothing wrong with these, but the Bible makes it clear that none of them can earn us God's forgiveness or re-establish our relationship with Him."

Then I draw a couple of arrows, going over the "Us" cliff. These signify our attempts to reach God that always fall short. Sometimes, I'll write "Romans 3:23" next to the arrows so the person can see the biblical source for what I'm saying.

"Furthermore," I add, "the sins we've committed must be punished, and the penalty we owe is death, which means physical death as well as spiritual separation from God for eternity, in a place called hell." Here I add the word "Death", and sometimes Romans 6:23, at the bottom of the chasm:

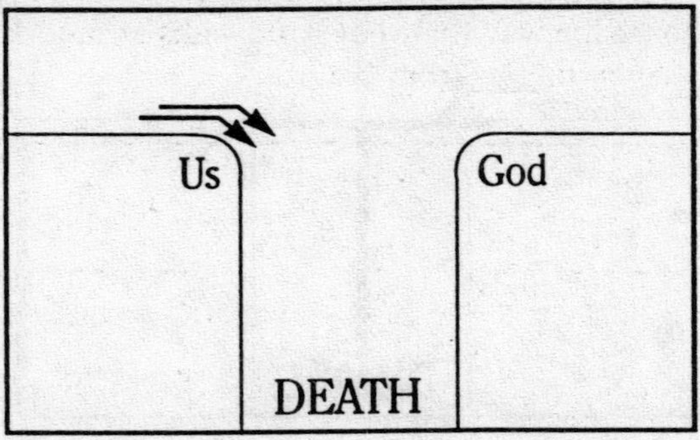

At this point, I admit that the picture looks pretty bleak. It's important to convey the reality of how much trouble we're in apart from Christ. People need to realise how lost they are before they're likely to become interested in being found.

But I don't leave them hanging on the bad news for too long. "The good news, as I said at the beginning, is that we matter to God. In fact, He loves us so much that He did for us what we could never do for ourselves. He provided a bridge over which we can find His forgiveness and restore our relationship with Him. He built it by coming to earth as one of us, and dying on the cross to pay the death penalty we owed. Here's what the bridge looks like."

Then I draw a cross in such a way that it touches both sides of the chasm, and sometimes I add "1 Peter 3:18" next to the cross (see top of following page).

"That," I conclude, "is a picture of what the central message of the Bible is all about. And that's what God wants each of us to understand. But it's not enough for us to just know about this or even agree with it. We've got to act upon it. God wants us to move over to the other side.

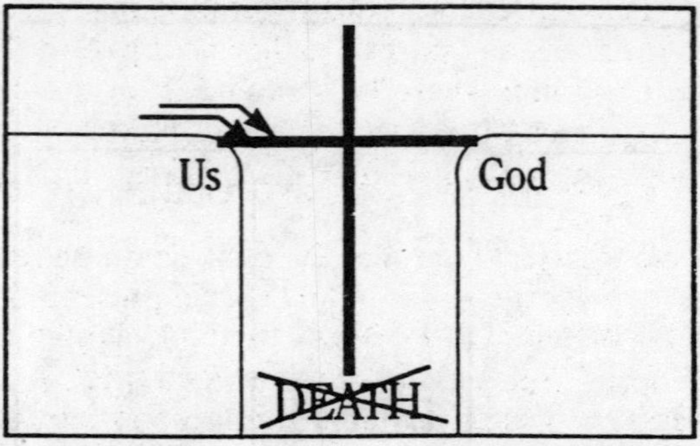

"We do this by humbly admitting to God that we've rebelled against Him and need His forgiveness and leadership. That simple act of trust and obedience results in our sins being pardoned and our debt being paid. Our relationship with God is firmly established, because we're immediately adopted into His family as His son or daughter."

While explaining this, I draw a stick figure on the "Us" side of the chasm, and then from it an arrow over the bridge to another stick figure on the "God" side, sometimes adding "John 1:12":

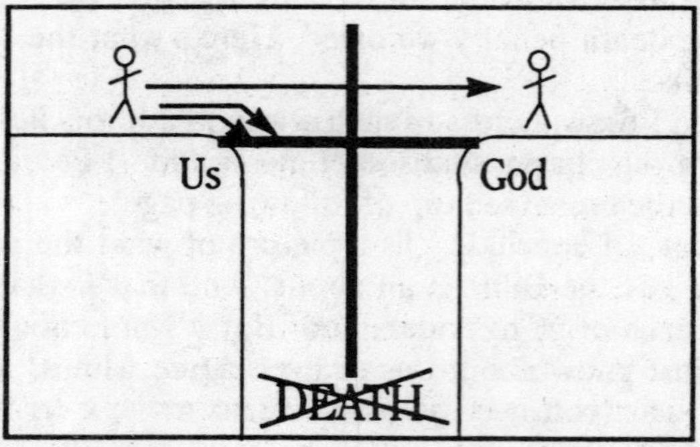

Then I ask my friend if the illustration makes sense to him or if there's any part of it that he'd like to discuss. Finally, I ask him where he'd say he is on the drawing and, if he seems open, whether he'd like to move over the bridge by making Christ his forgiver, leader, and friend.

Let me interject here that the most common response people make at this point in any gospel presentation is a heartfelt, "Hmmm . . . I'll have to think about it for a while." That's okay. Most seekers need time to process the message, weigh its implications, and consider its cost, just as Jesus suggested in Luke 14:28–33.

Sometimes God does a miracle and instantaneously changes a Saul into a Paul, but that's the exception and not the rule. At other times, He's already prepared the person through the efforts of somebody else. But as a general rule people need time to think it over.

We need to give them that freedom. If we push or rush them, they'll back out of the process. But if we allow them to move at their own pace, we'll be able to help them gradually progress until, eventually, God brings them to the point of crossing the bridge and trusting Christ.

The Roman road

This is one of the most effective presentations for people who've heard the message but need to see it in black and white, right out of the pages of the Bible. It's based on three verses in the book of Romans. I'd suggest underlining these in your Bible so that they're easy to find and show to others.

The first verse to show your friends is Romans 3:23, "For all have sinned and fall short of the glory of God." I explain, "According to this, all of us have sinned against God. This includes not only big sins, like rape and murder, but also stuff like moral missteps, lies, cruelty, insensitivity toward others, losing your temper, cheating, and self-centredness. I'm willing to admit to some of these. How about you?" Most people have no trouble admitting they've done these things, too.

Then I turn to the second verse, Romans 6:23, and let them read, "For the wages of sin is death, but the gift of God is eternal life in Christ Jesus our Lord." I'll say, "According to this verse, those little wrongdoings you and I just admitted to have earned us a penalty. The penalty is death."

When someone shows some interest in your faith, it doesn't necessarily mean they want all the details. Initially, most people merely want the Cliff Notes version.

But then I'll draw attention to the second half of the verse, and say, "It refers here to a gift. God has offered us a gift of eternal life. We can freely receive God's forgiveness and His pardon from the death penalty that we owed. The penalty has been paid for by Jesus' death on the cross. And like any other gift, we can't earn it, we can only receive it. To find out how, let's turn to one more verse." And then I'll let the person read Romans 10:13, where it says, "Everyone who calls on the name of the Lord will be saved."

"Do you see how simple it is to receive God's gift? All we have to do is recognise the fact that we've sinned and deserve death, and then call out to God humbly for His forgiveness and the new life He's offering us. That's what I did a few years back, and I'd like to encourage you to do the same."

The football illustration

This one is good for sports fans who need to be convinced that their moral efforts can never gain them salvation.

I describe a new honour being offered to the top football players. I call it the "All-Universe Hall of Fame". The prestige and rewards for being inducted are astronomical. There are only three requirements for entrance, and they're easy to understand.

First, the person must play consistently for at least five consecutive years. Second, they must play error-free ball. That's right—no errors, ever. And third, they must score at least one goal every game. Just do those three things, and you're automatically assured induction into the All-Universe Hall of Fame!

Simple? Yes, and obviously impossible, too. This is what the Bible says about trying to earn your way into heaven. Romans 3:23 makes it clear that no matter how hard we try, we'll always fall short of God's standard. In fact, James 2:10 says, "For whoever keeps the whole law and yet stumbles at just one point is guilty of breaking all of it."

Thank God that what we could never do for ourselves, He has already done for us. Jesus came to earth and, in effect, played error-free ball and scored a goal every game. Like a relief player who is substituting for us, He lived a perfect life on our behalf and then died to pay the penalty for our sins. And all we have to do is receive Him and His gift.

The aeroplane illustration

This is a good tool for helping complacent seekers and nominal church-goers understand that it's not enough to merely believe the right things about God or to just attend church.

Doing those things is like studying the science of aviation and then hanging around in airports. You can learn all about the physics of flight, know which airlines have the safest record, pick the best craft to fly in, reserve your flight, drive to the airport, go to the gate, double check the cockpit crew's credentials. But it does you no good unless you get on the plane.

Knowledge alone won't get you anywhere. You have to act on what you know. You have to climb aboard the aeroplane, trusting it'll take you where you want to go.

Similarly, it's not enough to know all about Christianity. You can study until you're an expert, go to church, even get involved in ministry, and not have a relationship with Christ. You finally have to take a step of faith and "get on board" by receiving the forgiveness He purchased on the cross and entrusting your life and future to Him. *That's* what it means to become a real Christian.

Your personal story

There's a final method of presentation that I need to mention, and I've saved one of the best for last. It's your personal account of how God has changed your life. We touched on this approach briefly when we discussed the testimonial style, but the fact is that *all* believers have a story to tell.

People enjoy hearing other people's stories. A concise and well-thought-out description of your own journey to faith can have a powerful effect on your listeners. It's hard to argue with. If your life demonstrates the kind of contagious character we discussed in section two, it'll make them want to know what's behind it.

Here's an example of how you can use your story. Let's say you have a friend at work named Barbara.

You've been hanging out together and have a fairly close friendship. You pray for her regularly.

With love in your heart, take a deep breath, look them in the eye, say it to them straight, and see where God takes it.

In the course of conversation, you find out that Barbara thinks she's a Christian, though based on her lifestyle you're pretty confident she's not serious about it. So over lunch one day, you sense the Holy Spirit prompting you, and you say something like this: "You know, Barbara, for most of my life, I thought I was a Christian because of my religious background. I was baptised and confirmed when I was young, attended services regularly, gave a little financial support, and helped out here and there. On top of that I tried to live a decent, moral life.

"But what I found out, Barbara, is that those things don't make you a Christian. It's like going to the Olympics. Just being there doesn't make you an athlete. But then a few years back I found out what a real Christian is, and I became one. If you'd ever like to hear more about what that means, I'd be happy to explain it to you, because it was the most important decision of my life."

Now, that example would only take a minute or two. It's simple and personal without being pushy or accusatory. The ball is now in Barbara's court. If she tells you she's interested, you can continue by telling her more about your experience and by using some of the other gospel illustrations I've described. If not, that's okay. Maybe she'll become more open at a later date. At least you've planted seeds for future conversations.

The personal story is a tool the apostle Paul used three different times in the book of Acts. I've used it numerous times myself. And I encourage you to put some thought into how you can best convey your story, too. Write it out and practice saying it, not for the purpose of memorising and retelling it word-for-word, but so that you can get comfortable with the basics of what you want to convey. Don't make it long or complicated. Just hit the high points of God's activity in your life in a way that will be relevant to your friends.

Then tell it to others—and watch God work through it.

Communication tips

As we close this chapter, here are a few general tips to make your presentation more effective, however you design it.

Don't give a speech

People want to talk *with* you, not be talked at *by* you. Sometimes when we get an opportunity to talk about our faith, we get a little excited and blurt out a monologue of whatever we think they need to hear. But now that you're aware of that danger, do whatever you can to prevent it.

The best way to avoid shifting into speech-mode is to ask questions first and then listen attentively to the answers. Then when it's your turn to talk, watch the other person to see if they're following you. If they look confused, stop and ask them whether what you're saying makes sense to them. Get their perspective on the matter. In so doing, you'll lower the tension, show respect for the other person, learn more about what they believe, and earn the right to express more of your thoughts.

Give it in doses

Another problem we might encounter is giving too much information at once. Someone said Christians have two problems when it comes to communicating their faith: starting and stopping! Well, our last chapter was on getting started, and I want to emphasise now that sometimes the best thing you can do is to stop.

When someone shows some interest in your faith, it doesn't necessarily mean they want all the details. Initially, most people merely want the *Cliff Notes* version. Over time, however, their curiosity may grow and their interest expand in spiritual matters.

But until that happens, we must give them just enough to satisfy their thirst—whether that takes a minute or an hour—and then back off. This will let them know it's easy to get in and out of discussions with us and keep them coming back for more information.

I believe that people will respect you for not beating around the bush. They're looking for something that makes sense, and they want to hear it from someone who really believes what they're saying.

Be bold

Finally, when you've prepared and prayed for opportunities, the moment will come. And I'll make a prediction: You probably won't feel ready or fully up to the task. I rarely do either.

That's when you lean on the strength and wisdom that the Holy Spirit provides. With love in your heart, take a deep breath, look them in the eye, say it to them straight, and see where God takes it.

I believe that people will respect you for not beating around the bush. They're looking for something that makes sense, and they want to hear it from someone who really believes what they're saying.

That person can be *you*.

> How, then, can they call on the one they have not believed in? And how can they believe in the one of whom they have not heard? And how can they hear without someone preaching to them? (Romans 10:14)

CHAPTER TWELVE

Breaking the Barriers to Belief

"Just give it up, would you? What do you take me for anyway, a *fool*? I'd have to push my finger into the wounds in His hands and His feet, and stick my arm into His side all the way up to my elbow before I'd ever believe He was raised from the dead.

"You can fantasise all you want to about a resurrection," Thomas continued, "but it looks to me like I've already wasted three years of my life. I'm not going to give up one more day on anything associated with Jesus. Don't you get it? It's *over*!"

The disciples were huddled together in a house trying to make sense of recent events. A few days after Thomas's tirade, Jesus suddenly appeared in the middle of the room. It soon became obvious that He wasn't there just to have some Christian fellowship. He carefully looked around the room, as if to find a certain person.

Then He locked eyes with Thomas.

When I let my imagination run wild, I'm reminded of those old western movies where two men square off in a saloon. While they're staring each other down, everyone else starts diving behind tables and chairs to make themselves scarce because they know there's going to be some action.

Well, I can just picture Jesus squaring off with Thomas. And I can imagine the other disciples, remembering Thomas's diatribe a few days earlier, clearing out of the way. My guess is they were thinking, *Is he ever going to get it. He's going to regret ever opening his big mouth.*

Fearing the worst, they covered their eyes as Jesus walked up to within a foot of Thomas. The room because deathly quiet. And then they heard Jesus say two words: "Touch me."

Not "Beat it," or "Drop dead," or "Get lost." Not even "Straighten up." No, nothing remotely like that. Just "Touch me."

Those words communicated volumes about the character of Christ. Thomas and the other disciples learned a lot about Jesus that day. And the lesson was one that many of our friends need today.

A divine perspective

We've got to help people understand that God isn't angry or afraid of honest doubt from those who are trying to discover the truth about Him. In fact, He warmly invites any and all who have sincere questions to come, to seek, and to ask, because He wants to help them clear up the haze. Part of our challenge is to assist them in seeing how different Jesus is from the wild-eyed religious leaders in our world who demand blind loyalty from their followers and who disqualify anyone who has the audacity to doubt them. These self-appointed gurus try to manipulate and intimidate unsuspecting people into joining their cause.

With disarming deference to our human tendency to doubt, Jesus simply says, "Touch me. Do whatever it takes in order to find out I'm real."

This is welcome news to the friends and acquaintances

to whom you're trying to clarify the gospel. As they go through the process of considering a commitment to Christ, they'll inevitably experience waves of uncertainty about the whole proposition.

We've got to help people understand that God isn't angry or afraid of honest doubt from those who are trying to discover the truth about Him. In fact, He warmly invites any and all who have sincere questions to come, to seek, and to ask, because He wants to help them clear up the haze.

We can expect that to happen, and when it does, we should respond by emulating Jesus. We must not try to shame or hurry them through their confusion. Rather, we should walk with them through their doubts, empathising along the way with what they're thinking and feeling, and offering answers when it seems appropriate.

This is all part of the final element in the front half of our equation—clear communication, which starts with spiritual conversations. Eventually, these dialogues open into opportunities to explain and illustrate the gospel. But in the time between first understanding the message and later committing to Christ, our friends need assurance of the truthfulness of Christianity and what the implications are for their life.

So don't be dismayed when your seeking friends express doubts along the way. It's actually a positive sign. It shows that they have some genuine interest in the truth they're so carefully scrutinising.

Barriers to belief

Let's look at some of the stumbling blocks that keep people from faith: misperceptions, intellectual road-blocks, and moral misgivings. Key in on the ones you think might be issues for the people you're trying to reach.

Misperceptions

"If you commit your life to following Jesus Christ, you can take your freedom, your individuality, your sense of adventure, and any hopes you have for fulfilment in this life, and kiss them all goodbye. After all, you're signing up to join a bunch of lobotomised, look-alike, act-alike losers who have nothing better to do with their lives.

"But that's not *you*. You've got brains, talent, and potential. You have places to go, things to do, and goals to achieve. So whatever you do, stop this foolish talk about falling into line and becoming religious. This is the only life you'll ever have!"

I have a feeling I'm not the only one who's ever heard that voice. I'll bet it's familiar to you, too. More importantly, some of your unbelieving friends hear it playing inside their heads like an endless-loop tape recording.

The irony is that this message is the exact opposite of the truth about the Christian life and, at a deeper level, the truth about the nature and characteristics of God. As long as people cling to distorted images of God, they'll be severely limited in their motivation to seek Him. That's because our made-up pictures of God can never come close to the reality of what He's actually like.

So, where do these misperceptions come from and what can we do to counter them? I think they come from several sources: poor examples, bad teaching, and natural fears. We'll look at each of these, together with some suggested ways to respond.

Poor examples

Most of us have been around some naive, narrow-minded, and pessimistic people who—in the name of God, the Bible, or the church—condemn anything they don't happen to like. They toss around Bible verses and give two-pence answers to million-pound questions. And they're proud to tell those around them about all the awful things that they don't ever do.

The typical seeker responds with sarcasm. "You mean, if I want to become a serious Christian, I've got to be brain-dead? I've got to put on blinkers, become simplistic, and close my eyes to the realities of life? Wow, where do I go to sign up?"

What can you do to remove this barrier? First, let your friends know that you understand their hesitations. Try verbalising some of these fears yourself, like I just did. Tell them about the ill-founded worries you once had about following God. It's disarming for them to hear you voicing their concerns, especially ones they thought you'd never understand. It lets them know you're on their wavelength, that you realise that some Christians are off-base in their beliefs and behaviour. And it puts you in position to paint a more accurate picture of the Christian life.

Second, live your life as a model that shatters their stereotypes and gives them a new view of Christianity. Although your works can go a long way toward softening their prejudices, it's what you *do* that will ultimately reshape their perceptions. Your example can become the living illustration that breaks this barrier by convincing them that Christians favour love over law-keeping, truth over trivialities, and faith over frenetic religious activity.

In addition, anything you can do to get those friends around other authentic Christians will be energy well spent. They need to see that you are not the exception, but one of many who are living exciting lives through Christ.

Bad teaching

Many people carry around inaccurate portrayals of God because, formally or informally, they've been taught wrong ideas.

And as long as God is pictured as a helpless old man, a harsh ogre, a disinterested deity, or a cosmic killjoy, who in their right mind is going to get all worked up about knowing Him? Misguided mental images effectively blunt people's motivation to move toward God.

Again, we need to identify with our friends' concerns. You can do this by reflecting on your own former misconceptions, or by referring to ones you've seen in others, and then explaining how these can stymie our spiritual progress. I like the way Jay Kesler drives this home. He says to the person, "Tell me about the God you don't believe in. Maybe I don't believe in Him, either!" Ultimately, the only effective antidote for countering bad teaching is to correct it with good teaching, replacing misguided ideas with accurate ones. And the best way to do that is to teach the Bible and challenge people to study it for themselves. They'll discover that God's revelation about Himself is surprisingly different from the misperceptions people harbour about Him.

Another way to help friends adjust their view of God is to encourage them to read books that faithfully portray His character as it's revealed in the Bible. I'd recommend such classics as, *Your God is Too Small*, by J. B. Phillips, and *Knowing God*, by J. I. Packer. Also, Le Strobel's recent book, *What Jesus Would Say*, will give them a fresh and perhaps unexpected perspective on how God might interact with a number of well-known people today.

As long as God is pictured as a helpless old man, a harsh ogre, a disinterested deity, or a cosmic killjoy, who in their right mind is going to get all worked up about knowing Him? Misguided mental images effectively blunt people's motivation to move toward God.

Natural fears

When considering a life-changing choice, it's only natural to hesitate as we approach the point of decision. If this is true of buying a house or getting married, it's certainly all the more true when it comes to signing our lives over to someone else—even when that someone is God! Our natural fears and worries can blur the picture of what it is we're considering.

Underlying many people's distorted images of Christianity is the misperception that they're going to lose more than they'll ever gain. I had a conversation a while back with a man who was wrestling with this very issue. Finally, he said in an exasperated voice, "I understand the message, and it's starting to make a lot of sense. But before I make a commitment, you've got to tell me: What is God's agenda for my life *after* I take that step? I know what He says He's going to do for me in *eternity*, but what can I expect *right now*, between here and heaven?"

I could see that he was worked up about this, so I decided to respond by shocking him into seeing what he was really saying. I shot back, "All right, I'll tell you what God's agenda is. He is going to lock you up in a monastery with a bunch of meditating monks and throw away the key! He's going to wrap you up in a straight jacket of rules and regulations so tight you won't be able to breathe! He might just make you be a missionary—in Iraq!" His smile told me he realised that I was merely making a point.

Then I challenged him with a couple of questions: "What kind of God do you think He is? And why are you so sure that He's more of a taker than a giver?"

People who worry that they're going to give up more for God than they'll gain are underestimating His character. They're selling Him short. They need to know what it says in Psalm 34:8: "Taste and see that the LORD is good; blessed is the man who takes refuge in him."

In essence, the Bible says that being a Christian is not only a great way to die, but it's also the best way to live. We need to help our friends understand this so they can overcome their natural fears.

Jesus dealt with the same issues in His day. John 10 tells about a time when He sensed that the people around Him were worried about God's plan for their lives. So He said, in effect, "There's been enough confusion on this subject. I want to clear this up once and for all: The evil one comes to destroy your life. But I'm not like him. I came so that you could find life and experience it in all its fullness."

In essence, the Bible says that being a Christian is not only a great way to die, but it's also the best way to live. We need to help our friends understand this so they can overcome their natural fears.

Intellectual roadblocks

A second kind of barrier to belief is intellectual roadblocks: questions and objections that cause doubts about the veracity of Christianity.

Don't ever sweep these issues under the rug. It's very damaging for someone seeking the truth to have their queries about the faith taken lightly by a committed Christian. And it's even worse when that believer spiritualises his lack of knowledge by telling the seeker they'll "just have to take it on faith."

When we take that tack we're directly disobeying God's command in 1 Peter 3:15, which says, "Be prepared to give an answer to everyone who asks you to give the reason for the hope that you have." As the late Walter Martin warned, if we fail to come through with a rational response, we risk becoming just another excuse for that person to disbelieve.

Take your friend's questions and objections seriously. Thank God that they're interested and engaged enough to raise such important issues, and do your best to give them a worthy response.

You won't always have the answer on the tip of your tongue. In many cases the best thing you can do is tell them they've asked a good question and that, right now, you don't have a great answer. Assure them you'll do some homework and then get back to them. In the long run they might be more impressed that you put the work into checking it out and following up than they would have been if you'd had an answer in the first place.

When I see people challenging the Christian faith on intellectual grounds, I do two things. First, I try to help them realise the bankruptcy of the competitors to the faith—whatever they may be. Secondly, I try to help them see by contrast the superiority of the biblical position.

I hope you know we've got nothing to fear from the teaching of competing worldviews. To bolster confidence in that fact, I taught a series at our church called, "Alternatives to Christianity". In it I contrasted some of the claims of the New Age movement, cults, and world religions with those of the Bible. More recently, our church hosted a public debate between leading spokesmen for atheism and Christianity. These helped those in attendance make informed comparisons, and many of them made commitments to Christ.

It's easy to look on the surface of the alternative positions and be drawn to them. But the closer you look, the weaker they become. And the deeper you delve into the evidence for Christianity, the more your faith will grow. We must do our homework in order to firmly fix our own convictions. Then we need to do all we can to help our friends grapple with the truth and make it their own.

Here are a few examples of intellectual dilemmas your friends may face and some ways you might help to resolve them.

The historical accuracy of the Bible

We must show them the wealth of ancient writings, from both religious and secular sources, that support the reliability of the Christian Scriptures, as well as the many confirming finds of modern archaeological research.

In addition, they need to know that other faiths sorely lack this kind of historical credibility. For instance, contrary to the written record for eyewitnesses, Islamic teachings say that Jesus never even claimed to be the Son of God, and most modern Muslims deny the documented fact that Jesus died on the cross. And Mormonism teaches that advanced civilisations existed in the Americas at the time of Christ, a claim for which there is no reliable historical or archaeological evidence.

The logic of faith

The rationality of our faith has been affirmed and reaffirmed by many of the greatest minds throughout history. In fact, some of the strongest defenders of the faith started out as sceptics, studying in order to disprove Christianity, and in the process became believers.

In contrast, many of our friends who are concerned about this question would be surprised to find out that teachers of Eastern religions routinely argue against the validity of logic itself!

The problem of evil

Our friends need to realise that if the biblical accounts of human origins, freedom, and rebellion against God are true, the world should look a lot like what we see each night on the six o'clock news. There's nothing logically incompatible between the existence of an all-powerful Creator and moral rebellion in the world, especially in light of the fact that He promises to ultimately judge all evil.

The bigger challenge is for those who say that everything is God, as is taught in Eastern religions and the New Age movement. How can they make sense of or find hope in the inescapable conclusion that evil is therefore actually a *part* of God?

And the atheist position is no better, because without God, there is no objective standard of right and wrong; nothing is really evil, but merely distasteful to some individuals. But if all we're left with is personal taste, then who's to say that murder or rape are inherently wrong?

Christianity refutes these claims and affirms that evil is real, that it's not part of God, that it's against His standards and therefore wrong, and that we're accountable for what we do. That may not tell us everything we'd like to know about the subject, but what it does tell us makes a whole lot of sense.

Christianity vs. science

While the Bible was not written to be a textbook on science, its teachings display divine insight and truth when it touches on issues of a scientific nature. And its freedom from the folklore and mythological musings within so many other religious writings is impressive.

In addition, many people will find it interesting that increasing numbers of top-notch biologists, geologists, paleontologists, and astronomers are finding evidence for a divine Creator in the phenomena of the physical world. Good science and good theology point to the same truths about reality.

Take your friend's questions and objections seriously. Thank God that they're interested and engaged enough to raise such important issues, and do your best to give them a worthy response.

Hurdling the roadblocks

We need to help people see that while Christians have questions to deal with, those in the alternative camps have conundrums from which there's no logical escape. After studying the other options carefully, seeker after honest seeker comes to the conclusion that it takes more faith to *deny* Christianity than it does to actually *embrace* it.

So we've got to encourage our spiritually inquisitive friends to ask their questions and raise their doubts, but then to do their homework, consider the evidence, examine the Bible, read the books, look at history, weigh the facts, and listen to knowledgeable people who've devoted their lives to determining the validity of the Christian faith.

We can help our friends by pointing them toward some of the many books and tapes available by leading defenders of the faith, such as Josh McDowell, J. P. Moreland, William Lane Craig, Hugh Ross, Gary Habermas, Bob and Gretchen Passantino, Norman Geisler, Ravi Zacharias, Walter Martin, Paul Little, C. S. Lewis, and others. Most of these aren't household names, but considering how they've helped people break through their intellectual roadblocks, they ought to be.

Once our friends have done their research and weighed the facts, we need to encourage them to act on what they've found. This means not lying to themselves about their findings, or hiding behind the excuse that they haven't answered every possible question. Remind them that a jury has to finally reach a verdict based on the evidence they have available.

I once had a fascinating talk with an atheist friend. At the end of our long and lively discussion, he said, "Well, Bill, you believe one way and I see it another way. So why don't we just agree to disagree, and leave it at that?"

"But, Keith," I said, "there's a day coming—and it won't be long—when we're both going to find out who is right. We're banking our lives and destinies on totally contradictory ideas. We can't both be right. One of us is going to hit the jackpot and the other is going to be in remorse for eternity. Keith, I've done my homework on this subject, but I really wonder if you've done yours. Why not deal with your doubts directly, and make sure you've found the right answers?"

That's what Thomas did. He doubted, too. But he also weighed the evidence and ended up falling before

Jesus and saying those heart-felt words found in John 20:28: "My Lord and my God!" He believed, based on the facts, just as thousands of truth-seekers have done since then.

Moral misgivings

"That was a pretty good talk you just gave, but I can't accept the Christian position because there are too many logical holes in it."

"That's interesting," replied Mark, "because I haven't discovered them yet. What issues bother you?"

It was difficult to tell which of them was more excited about this conversation. For the next forty-five minutes this man threw his challenges at Mark. And Mark, in turn, drew from his background in theology and apologetics to answer the objections, as well as to confront this man with the truth of the gospel.

When the smoke cleared, Mark sensed there was something deeper going on. So he looked the man in the eye and said, "You are raising some good questions, but I want to know what the *real* issue is. What are you so afraid of having to change or give up if you commit your life to Christ?"

To his surprise, the man vulnerably admitted that there were moral issues in his life that he didn't want to deal with. "That, I'm afraid, is your *real* question," declared Mark. "And until you're willing to let God change that area of your life, you'll keep finding every excuse in the book to write off Christianity."

I've seen this sort of thing for years. Some seekers have serious intellectual questions that are preventing their progress toward Christ. Others just act like that's their situation, and they use philosophical-sounding objections in an effort to keep the focus off of their ordinary, old-fashioned sin.

What often happens is that the person will lead off

with a couple of honest questions. But when he sees that there are good answers, he gets nervous. That's when he has to make a choice. He can either open up and be honest, like the man Mark spoke with above, or he can start raising every random issue that comes to his mind in order to keep you—and God—at arm's length.

While Christians have questions to deal with, those in the alternative camps have conundrums from which there's no logical escape. After studying the other options carefully, seeker after honest seeker comes to the conclusion that it takes more faith to deny Christianity than it does to actually embrace it.

When you sense that someone is putting up a smoke-screen, my advice is to come right out and call his bluff. Tell him frankly that he seems to be putting more energy into finding questions than answers, and ask whether he's afraid God will want to change him or make him give up something to follow Christ. If he divulges that there is, you then have the chance to help him determine how valuable that thing really is.

In other words, assist him in a cost-benefit analysis. For example, if the person admits he enjoys spending his weekends getting out of control on alcohol, and he's unwilling to give that up to follow God, you've now got something to measure. With his cooperation, you can put that issue on a written or mental chart, and help him take an honest look at what he's gaining and what he's losing by hanging on to it.

"Okay," you might start, "let's list all the things getting drunk does for you. We'll get more sheets of paper, by the way, if we need them. You talk and I'll write."

"It tastes good," he begins, "and it's fun. Besides, all my friends are into it."

"Great. What else?" Silence. "Anything else?" you ask again. He's already scraping, "...and...uhhh, it helps me relax."

"All right, if you think of any more benefits, we'll add them to the page. Now let's look at the downside. You don't mind if I help you think of some things, do you?" And in short order you'll have a long list of items like:

- I end up saying and doing things I later regret.
- My hangovers are downright painful.
- It costs me good money, not to mention time and energy.
- I'm risking eventual liver disease (or at least a beer belly!).
- There's a high probability of alcohol addiction.
- It impairs my ability to drive, which risks not only property, but also could cost somebody their life.

This kind of evaluation means even more when you point out to your friend how much he matters to God. Explain that God cares so much about him that He's trying to prevent him from all of these problems. He'll get a glimpse of what a kind and caring God we have.

And we haven't even looked yet at all the benefits he'll forfeit by not following Christ. When you add the lists of short- and long-term ways God blesses our lives to the analysis you've already done, there's simply no contest.

This approach can be helpful when applied to any area that a person is unwilling to give up. I'm not saying that they'll look at this simple calculation and make their decision purely on the data. But it can be an effective eye-opener that helps them eventually break through this barrier of moral misgivings as the Holy Spirit pulls them toward Christ.

Breaking the barriers

The process may be short or it may be long, but we've got to stick with it, helping our friends clear away whatever barriers are standing between them and Christ.

Along the way, we can encourage them by pointing out two things: a prayer and a promise. The prayer is found in Mark 9, where a man had asked Jesus to heal and deliver his son. Jesus told him it would be possible, if he would just believe. To this the man replied, in verse 24, "I do believe; help me overcome my unbelief!"

I find two interesting things about this "doubter's prayer." First, Jesus did not put down the man for wavering in his faith. And secondly, He actually went ahead and answered His prayer anyway! That tells us a lot about God, and it gives us great insight into how we can approach Him.

I'll often encourage a seeking friend to take whatever faith he can muster, as well as all of the doubts he's facing, and just talk to God openly about them. I've led people in prayers along those lines, encouraging them to express their mixed-up feelings to God. They'll say things like, "God, I'm not even sure you're there. But if you are, I'd sure like you to let me know. If you're real, I want to know you."

That, I believe, is a prayer God takes seriously. Which leads to the promise. Jesus states in Matthew 7:7–8, "Ask and it will be given to you; seek and you will find; knock and the door will be opened to you. For everyone who asks receives; he who seeks finds; and to him who knocks, the door will be opened."

And in Jeremiah 29:13, God said, "You will seek me

and find me when you seek me with all your heart." Though this was addressed to a certain group of people at a specific time in history, I think it informs us how to coach our friends concerning Jesus' promise about asking, seeking, and knocking. Namely, they need to do it whole-heartedly. To make it a front-burner issue. To realise that the ramifications of this decision are so great that it warrants top-priority.

If they'll sustain that kind of an all-out effort, they're going to break through all the barriers keeping them from belief. It's an incredible privilege to help someone through this process, and then eventually to usher them across the line of faith, as they embrace Christ as their forgiver, leader, and friend. We'll explore how you can do this in the next chapter, where we'll begin the section on maximum impact.

Kerry Livgren described the searching process poignantly in his powerful song, "The Wall". He wrote these words while still a spiritual seeker, several years before he became a Christian:

> I'm woven in a fantasy, I can't believe the things I see
> The path that I have chosen now has led me to a wall
> And with each passing day I feel a little more like something dear was lost
> It rises now before me, a dark and silent barrier between,
> All I am, and all that I would ever want to be
> It's just a travesty, towering, marking off the boundaries my spirit would erase
>
> To pass beyond is what I seek, I fear that I may be too weak

And those are few who've seen it through to
glimpse the other side,
The promised land is waiting like a maiden that is
soon to be a bride
The moment is a masterpiece, the weight of
indecision's in the air
It's standing there, the symbol and the sum of all
that's me
It's just a travesty, towering, blocking out the light
and blinding me
I want to see

Gold and diamonds cast a spell, it's not for me I
know it well
The treasures that I seek are waiting on the other
side
There's more than I can measure in the treasure
of the love that I can find
And though it's always been with me, I must tear
down the wall and let it be
All I am, and all that I was ever meant to be, in
harmony
Shining true and smiling back at all who wait to
cross
There is no loss*

SECTION FIVE

The Payoff: Maximum Impact

HP + CP + CC = *MI*

CHAPTER THIRTEEN

Crossing the Line of Faith

A few years ago a friend of mine stopped by the church to tell me he'd lost his job, and he wondered if I could do anything to help him. I told him I'd do my best. Later in the week I called another friend of mine who runs a business, and I took a risk: I played vocational cupid. As you might know, it doesn't usually work out very well. This time was no exception.

The friend who owned the business said, "Sure, if you think he's a good guy, send him my way. I need a new salesman." So I served as the liaison, and it seemed that everyone was happy. That is, until several months later, when I found out my buddy had been made redundant.

So the next time I happened to be talking to the business owner, I asked him why my friend didn't make it with his company. "Well," he said, "your friend was conscientious, aggressive, hard-working, and he could even make a decent sales presentation. . . ." He paused.

"Then what was the problem?" I asked.

"The man could never ask for the order! He'd get the clients in the room and make his pitch, but he seemed totally incapable of asking them to buy the product. What good is a salesman if he can't close a sale?"

Sometimes pastors from around the country will send me tapes of their messages and ask me for a critique. It's a process I'm very familiar with, because every time I speak at Willow Creek, there are four or five people who evaluate my preaching and give me written feedback in order to coach me on how I can do it better the next time.

Often I'll end up saying something like, "You had good content, clear points, strong illustrations, it was biblical, and you filled the whole thirty minutes." But then a lot of times I'll have to add, "But what did you want your people to *do*? If you had some hope or expectation about how they were supposed to let the message change them, it didn't come through." In effect, I'm telling them, "You forgot to ask for the order!"

You see, a good message helps people *understand* something, but it also inspires them to *do* something: to make a decision about an area of their life that really matters. The speaker needs to inform his or her listeners of a truth from God's Word and then say, "Take some action!"

We've been discussing how we can become contagious Christians: followers of Christ who develop highly potent character traits, who move into close proximity with those we want to reach, and who then communicate the gospel in a clear and compelling way. But if we stop there, we'll end up short of the full goal of the formula, which is MI, or *Maximum Impact*.

There are many believers who are frustrated in their efforts to spread the faith. They pray, set good examples in the way they live, and are sensitive in how they share the message. But they rarely see lives actually change because they stop right there. Somewhere along the line they've lost track of the objective and, as a result, fail to ask people to take action upon what they've heard.

So many Christians have gotten the mistaken idea that the goal of evangelism is just to tell more people about

Christ. "Oh," they say, "If I would take more opportunities to share the gospel with others, God would be pleased and I'd feel so much better."

But the goal is not merely to *tell* people about Christ. That's just the process we use to reach the goal, which is to *lead* people to Christ. Remember Jesus' words in The Great Commission in Matthew 28:19: "Therefore go and make disciples. . . ." The process of communicating the message is important, but it's the end product—forming new, growing believers—that Jesus emphasised.

So, like my friend who tried to make it in sales, we've got to get beyond just making presentations and start asking people for the order. Like some of the sermons I evaluate, we not only need to help our listeners understand, we also need to inspire and challenge them to do something: specifically, to step across the line of faith.

Beyond comparison

I like adventure. Sometimes I find it comes in fairly calm forms, like sailing boats or flying planes. And, I'll have to admit, at times I've found it in more intense forms, like jumping *out* of speedboats and skydiving.

But I've learned that there's no adventure like personally leading someone to a commitment to Christ. There's something amazing and unforgettable about being involved in the eternity-altering miracle that God Himself is doing in that person's life.

Right there in front of you, invisibly and yet assuredly, God is forgiving, transforming, indwelling, redirecting, and adopting your friend. And He used *you* as His principle instrument for making it all happen. I don't know about you, but I call that adventure!

But many believers never experience this ultimate goal of contagious Christianity because they need some pointers on how to finish the process. That's the purpose of this chapter: to explore practical ideas for how each of us can become more effective in helping friends take that life-changing step of faith in Christ. But before we get into the details, I'd like to disclaim a disclaimer.

You've heard the warning, "Caution: don't try this at home. The people you're about to see are trained professionals." Well, I'd like to turn it around for our topic and say, "*Do* try this at home, work, in a restaurant, or on a park bench. Don't wait around for trained professionals; they may never show up. Besides, your friends will trust you more anyway."

It's my prayer that at least once you'll feel the thrill of ushering someone you know into a relationship with Christ. Let's explore ways to make that happen.

The goal is not merely to tell people about Christ. That's just the process we use to reach the goal, which is to lead people to Christ.

Approaching the line

The first step in moving people toward the point of decision is to simply find out where they're at. You can do this by applying your message, whether it's one of the gospel illustrations or your personal story, to their spiritual situation. Ask something like, "So, have you ever come to the place of realising that you need to:

- give up on *doing* and start trusting what Christ has *done* on your behalf?"
- stop trying to get over the sin chasm by your own efforts, and cross over on the bridge that God has provided?"

- acknowledge the wages you've earned through sin, and receive the gift that is offered freely through Christ?"
- face up to the fact that you'll never play error-free ball, and ask Christ to substitute for you?"
- get beyond just studying about aviation, and actually climb aboard the aeroplane?"
- let go of the idea that going to church and being a good person will make you right with God, and ask Him to give you His gift of forgiveness and guidance for everyday living?"

These turning-point questions will shift the focus from you and your words to them and their standing with Christ. As they respond, you must assess their interest, their understanding, and their readiness so you can proceed accordingly.

Assessing interest

If your friends respond to your question in a defensive or disinterested fashion, continue the conversation with caution. They may be open to discussing why they reacted the way they did, and that can be extremely helpful information. But don't push too hard.

Sometimes the wisest thing you can do is to thank them for giving you the chance to explain something that's so important to you, and then ask them to mull it over for possible future discussions. Your willingness to back off can be the very thing that lowers their defences. They need to know that although you're enthusiastic about your faith, you're not a fanatic who'll drive the subject into the ground.

On the other hand, if your friends do show interest in hearing more, you're ready to move on to the next area.

Assessing understanding

Your friends' response to your question, along with the interaction that follows, will tell you a lot about their level of spiritual understanding. Some people will have a clear comprehension of the gospel, but they aren't ready to respond to it. Others are very open, and might even be willing to trust Christ, but they're still fuzzy on what the message really is. Diagnosing the difference is critically important.

Don't let the simplicity of the illustrations in chapter eleven fool you. The biblical message they spell out is such a radical departure from what most people believe that it usually takes a while to let it really sink in. In fact, I've found that most seekers require months of hearing it, processing it, questioning it, and considering it before they're ready to respond to it in a positive way.

Because of the difficulty many people have in grasping the message, it's important to have several different illustrations in your pocket. Some people won't click with bridges or aeroplanes, but football might just make sense to them. I often try out two or three angles, usually over a period of time, to help them see the real picture.

So be ready to say it again and again, sometimes putting it in fresh terms. And ask them to explain it back to you. Whether they're ready to commit to Christ or not, it's vitally important that they know exactly what it is they're supposed to be considering.

It's my prayer that at least once you'll feel the thrill of ushering someone you know into a relationship with Christ.

Assessing readiness

In the course of your conversations, you'll see at least a degree of openness in many people. They're willing to admit that they've never received—or, at least, that they're not sure they've ever received—the forgiveness and leadership of Christ.

Let me interject here the importance of asking God to give you an attitude of expectancy. Your words and actions need to communicate to them that knowing and serving God is what we were all created to do. You've chosen to commit your life to Him, scores of other people have done the same, and it's something they need to do, too. This message will foster confidence that this is the direction in which they ought to be moving.

Holy Spirit-inspired expectancy is what enables you to move on to the next step. In both my personal and public ministries I've often been tempted to stop short of offering people the opportunity to make a commitment to Christ. But then at the last minute I've sensed God prompting me to go ahead, and I've seen Him change lives as a result.

So what's the next step for those who seem ready? Ask another question: "Is there any reason you wouldn't want to pray with me right now to make certain you've received God's forgiveness and have become a member of His family?"

I like this approach because it's simple, and it leaves them with just two ways to respond. They can say yes, there is a reason to wait. Or they can say no, implying they're ready to proceed. Let's look into what we should do in both of these cases.

If they're not ready

If your friends are not open to receiving Christ, then it's only natural for you to ask why, in the hope that you can help them work through whatever the problem is. It might be that one of the barriers to belief we discussed in the last chapter is holding them back.

If so, you'll need to put time and effort into helping them break through that barrier. But that's okay. You're helping them deal with their real issues, so that down the line they can trust Christ. That assistance may take the form of providing resources that address their questions, setting aside time for further discussions, or just giving them a chance to think over this important decision.

I've often been tempted to stop short of offering people the opportunity to make a commitment to Christ. But then at the last minute I've sensed God prompting me to go ahead, and I've seen Him change lives as a result.

Here's another idea for those who aren't ready: Offer to pray for them and their spiritual progress right then and there, assuring them that you'll do the talking and they can just listen. If they say yes, they'll be taking a preliminary step in the right direction, and you'll know that God will hear and respond. And if they're open to verbalising a doubter's prayer to God, all the better!

In the last chapter we saw that there are natural fears a person faces as they near the point of decision. But sometimes those fears grow to unusually large proportions. When that happens, the problem might be that Satan is taking their concerns and turbocharging them. His greatest weapon is fear, so it only makes sense that he'd try to accentuate the anxiety people already feel.

If you think that might be happening, calmly explain

to the person that God has a spiritual enemy who, since the Garden of Eden, has whispered into people's ears all kinds of irrational ideas about what they have to lose, miss, or change to follow God. Once people are armed with an understanding of how the enemy works, it's easier for them to ignore his appeal.

It's a good idea to back up that explanation with a silent prayer for protection. Ephesians 6:12 says, "For our struggle is not against flesh and blood, but against the rulers, against the authorities, against the powers of this dark world and against the spiritual forces of evil in the heavenly realms." This is something to take seriously but not to be frightened by. Don't forget James 4:7–8, which says, "Submit yourselves, then, to God. Resist the devil, and he will flee from you. Come near to God and he will come near to you."

If they are ready

More often than you'd expect, however, people will respond positively to your question about trusting Christ. "No, I can't think of any reason I shouldn't take that step right now. How do I go about it?" they may say.

Unless you sense that there are other issues you ought to discuss, it's safe to assume that person is ready. And you'll need to be ready, too. Let's look at some practical approaches you can use.

Crossing the line

"I'm fairly new to the church," the man on the phone said to Mark, "and I'm interested in making an appointment to talk about some of the things that this Hybels person has been saying at the weekend services." It was a request Mark couldn't resist, so he set up a time to get together with Jim later in the week.

When they met, the gospel was expounded and explained, defined and defended, as Mark responded to the many questions Jim raised about the Christian faith. Finally, about an hour and a half later, Jim relaxed in his chair, and said, "I guess you've answered most of my questions. Now what do I do?"

Picture yourself in that situation. Are your knees knocking? Here are some guidelines to help you through the process.

Relax

Just as God has been guiding you in the conversations you've already had, He'll help you now to lead the person to faith. It's encouraging to realise that God has been working for a long time to bring the seeker to this point. He's not going to abandon the process now and let you make a fatal mistake that will ultimately mess them up!

Forget about word formulas

One of the things that makes Christians nervous in these situations is the feeling that they don't know the perfect prayer for leading people to Christ. They've watched Billy Graham say it on television, but they can't remember the words. They've read the prayer on the back page of gospel tracts, yet those things never seem to be around when you need them.

The truth is that there's no magic formula to worry about. All the person needs is an attitude of repentance, which means a desire to turn away from her sins, and a little help from you to make a heartfelt request to God for His salvation.

J. Allen Peterson tells about a man who was stuck in the middle of a New York city traffic jam, and the Holy Spirit was working on him. Finally, in exasperation, he blurted out to God: "All right, here I am—guts, feathers, and all. Take me!" And the man's life was transformed by Christ.

Think back to the words of the thief on the cross in Luke 23:40–43. He first defended Jesus' innocence, and then said to Him, "Jesus, remember me when you come into your kingdom." That was it! One single sentence. And Jesus replied, "I tell you the truth, today you will be with me in paradise."

Pray together

Seize the opportunity by suggesting that the two of you find a quiet place and talk to God about it right then. Since most seekers are sketchy about how to pray, they'll welcome your willingness to help them formally take that step. It also helps them feel more confident later to have you as a witness to the fact that, yes, they really did receive God's forgiveness and begin to follow Christ.

I should add that on rare occasions people will be adamant about going home to pray with the parent, spouse, or friend who has been a major spiritual influence on their life. You'd be wise to encourage them to do so that very evening, and then to call you the next day to let you know what happened. This will motivate them to follow through. Also, if they don't call you the next day, telephone them yourself either to hear the story or to challenge them not to further delay this important step.

Pray aloud

Primarily for reasons of clarity, I think it's best to pray together out loud. For one thing, you can hear what they're actually saying to God and help them in ways I'll describe below. And this is another way to help them know that they did, indeed, ask for God's forgiveness and leadership because they heard themselves say the words!

I've found that if you offer guidance, most people will be willing to pray out loud. This also sets the stage for their prayer life as a new believer. Tell them that they've done a great job of expressing their thoughts to you, so now they can just do the same toward God. Also, encourage them to continue to use plain language and not add thees, thous, or attempts at poetry. God likes to hear their own way of saying things.

It's encouraging to realise that God has been working for a long time to bring the seeker to this point. He's not going to abandon the process now and let you make a fatal mistake that will ultimately mess them up!

Lead off the prayer

Those things being understood, just bow your head and start the prayer in a natural tone that will model for them how they can talk to God. I'd begin by thanking Him for bringing them to this point, and asking Him to help them humbly and wholeheartedly receive His forgiveness and leadership.

Turn it over to them

Next, tell them to go ahead and talk to God in their own words. Encourage them to focus on two things: their need for God's forgiveness, which Christ paid for on the cross, and for His leadership. Then just listen.

It might take them a minute to get up the nerve to talk. But if you wait, they'll finally say a prayer from the heart which, in my experience, will be among the most authentic and moving prayers you'll ever hear.

It's important, however, that you monitor what they say to make sure they're on the right track. For instance, make certain they're praying an "I've sinned and need your grace" prayer, rather than an "I've been bad but I'm going to try harder" resolution. If you sense they're getting off course, interrupt gently and discuss it as necessary until you feel they're ready to continue.

If there's a particular area of sin that they've confided to you as being troublesome in their life, you may want to suggest they talk to God about it specifically, asking Him to forgive it and to help them overcome it.

Then, when you feel that they've adequately talked to God about forgiveness, prompt them to move on to the second area, which is God's leadership for their life. Encourage them to ask Christ to lead their life, and to ask for God's Spirit to come and change them from the inside out. Again, listen to what they pray. If necessary, add anything you think they need to hear or understand.

When that area seems to be covered, tell them there's one more thing to pray about. It relates to the two things they just asked for: God's forgiveness and His leadership. If they really meant what they prayed, He's already done it! So the third area is thanksgiving: expressing gratitude to God for the gifts He's just given them. Then enjoy listening as they say a heart-felt thanks.

Close the prayer

When they've finished thanking God, you'll find yourself quite naturally wanting to join in and thank Him, too. Don't hold back! It's appropriate for you, at this point, to enthusiastically praise God for the miracle He's just done in their life and for the joy you're feeling as a result. Then add a brief request that He'll protect and guide this new son or daughter through the exciting but challenging days of change that lie ahead.

Mark followed these steps in his conversation with Jim. The prayer only took a few minutes, but it was a faith transaction with God that put Jim's life on a whole new course. Now, several years later, he's still growing in his relationship with Christ and is active in our church.

This story could be told hundreds of times over, using different names. I just hope that very soon it will be told again, this time by you, and that the names of the new Christians will be your friends or family members. Their lives will be changed forever—and yours will, too.

Getting beyond the line

Of course, the Christian life doesn't end with the "Amen". Let's look briefly at what to do after the prayer to ensure that your friend gets established in his or her newfound faith.

Celebrate

After leading someone in a prayer of commitment, it's important to take some time to celebrate and talk about it. You may want to point out Luke 15:10: "There is rejoicing in the presence of the angels of God over one sinner who repents." This is an exciting moment, and your attitude should reflect it.

Of course, how people express their excitement will vary according to their personality. So don't be surprised if one time there are hugs and tears of joy, and another time the person just shakes your hand and says "thanks".

Affirm their commitment

It's important to reiterate the importance of what they've just done. Affirm that they have made the biggest decision of their life, and that they'll thank God for eternity. But be aware that some people won't feel deeply struck by the emotions you might have expected. That's okay. What matters is that they meant what they prayed. Feelings will follow, more strongly for some people than others.

Paint a realistic picture

Explain to them that there will be ups and downs in their level of intimacy with Christ and in the level of excitement they feel about serving Him. This is normal with any relationship or commitment. What's important is that they resolve to stay in communication with Him through thick and thin, both of which they're sure to experience.

Explain steps for spiritual growth

It's easy to overlook discussing basic habits that help us grow as Christians. But whether right on the spot or within the next day or two, it's vitally important to spend some time laying out practical suggestions about the following areas.

Prayer

Explain that they need to set aside a few minutes each day to communicate with God. Encourage them to keep talking to Him in everyday language, and to be honest and open about what's really on their mind each day. Even if they don't feel like praying, that's a good thing to tell God about!

To help maintain balance in prayer, I often tell people about the classic A-C-T-S outline. First, "A" stands for adoration; worshipping God is a great way to start. "C" is for confession; when they fall into a sin they need to admit to God, who affirms that they're forgiven. "T" is for thanksgiving, a natural response to His forgiveness and the many other signs of His love and care throughout their life. "S" is supplication, an older word that means to make requests; God wants us to do this and promises to hear and respond.

Praying together during subsequent meetings is an excellent way to illustrate the importance and reinforce the habit of talking to God.

Bible reading

Underscore the fact that the primary way God speaks to us is through His written revelation, the Bible. This was His letter to mankind, telling us about Himself, His love for us, the story of our sin and His salvation, and His guidelines for how we can serve and please Him.

Encourage a habit of reading a chapter each day, starting in one of the New Testament gospels, from a version of the Bible they can understand. Also, let them know ahead of time that they'll have questions as they go, and that they should jot them down and talk about them with you or another knowledgeable believer.

A book you might find useful for helping them establish balanced Bible study habits is *Living By the Book*, by Howard and William Hendricks.

Relationships with other Christians

Stress the importance of developing deep and honest friendships with other Christians and regularly spending time together. Those relationships will be an important source of encouragement, learning, and accountability.

Make sure they find a church that accurately and relevantly teaches from the Bible, and that fosters spiritual health and growth. Stress that the church is not only a place where they can be challenged and taught, but also a place where God wants to use them to serve others in a way that utilises the spiritual gifts He's given them. Inspire them with the fact that they're called to be important players on His team.

Relationships with non-Christians
It's never too early to let new believers know that God wants them to become contagious Christians, through whom He'll reach others. Share some of the principles you've learned about this, but also caution them to be patient with close friends and family members. These people will need time to watch them to see if the change in them is real before they'll seriously consider the implications of the gospel for themselves.

Provide long-term spiritual nurturing

The areas we've just covered provide an initial orientation to the Christian life, in order to get your friends off on the right foot. The problem is that too often we stop there, hoping that somehow they'll survive on their own. But knowing they're spiritual newborns, we've got to ensure that they receive proper spiritual nurturing. There are two good options for doing this. The first is natural parenting, and the second is adoption.

Knowing they're spiritual newborns, we've got to ensure that they receive proper spiritual nurturing. There are two good options for doing this. The first is natural parenting, and the second is adoption.

Natural parenting means that you, the person who led them across the line of faith, will take responsibility for meeting with them on a regular basis in order to disciple and encourage them. The advantage of this approach is that there's already a bond of trust between you, and it's natural to let that develop into the next phase of growth.

But often differences in age, personality, life-stage, gender, or location can make the second option—spiritual adoption—the better choice. This does not mean abandoning them at the door of some church. Rather, you need to carefully and prayerfully search out the right adoptive parent, a mature Christian with whom your friend has some affinity and who is willing to commit the time and energy needed to help them grow in their relationship with Christ.

As I said earlier, it's my prayer that you'll have the thrill, at least once, of personally leading a friend across the line of faith. It could be after just one or two conversations about spiritual matters, or it may take years of patient and prayerful effort. But when it finally happens, your faith and confidence and spiritual enthusiasm will grow, and it'll be that much easier to help someone else the next time. And along the way you'll become an increasingly contagious Christian.

To conclude this critically important topic, here's a challenging reminder from part of Sam Shoemaker's "So I Stay Near the Door".

I stay near the door.
I neither go too far in, nor stay too far out,
The door is the most important door in the
  world—
It is the door through which people walk when
  they find God.
There's no use my going way inside, and staying
  there,

When so many are still outside and they, as much as I,
Crave to know where the door is.
And all that so many ever find
Is only the wall where a door ought to be.
They creep along the wall like blind people,
With outstretched, groping hands,
Feeling for a door, knowing there must be a door,
Yet they never find it...
So I stay near the door.

The most tremendous thing in the world
Is for people to find that door—the door to God.
The most important thing anyone can do
Is to take hold of one of those blind, groping hands,
And to put it on the latch—the latch that only clicks
And opens to the person's own touch.
People die outside that door, as starving beggars die
On cold nights in cruel cities in the dead of winter—
Die for want of what is within their grasp.
They live, on the other side of it—live because they have found it.
Nothing else matters compared to helping them find it,
And open it, and walk in, and find Him...
So I stay near the door.

Just imagine the spiritual impact we'd have on the world if we had churches full of people doing just that. It's an exciting thought, one we'll expand on in the next chapter.

CHAPTER FOURTEEN

Contagious Christians and Contagious Churches

"You've got to be kidding!" Fred exclaimed. "*Me*—take a course in personal evangelism? I've got to tell you that of all the ways I've thought about spending my next few Tuesday nights, outreach training was definitely not one of them." Fred was almost dumbfounded that anyone would encourage him to consider such a thing.

But my friend persisted. "I'm just telling you I think you could be effective in spreading your faith to others and, besides, it would help you grow in your own understanding of Christianity."

Fred finally gave in. And, as it turned out, the course ignited a spiritual spark inside of him that hasn't gone out since. Almost immediately this man, who'd only been a Christian a short time, was actively communicating his faith to people he knew.

At first, he'd help friends get to the point of being ready to cross the line and then bring them to the church to let Mark or one of his other "coaches" help the person pray a prayer of commitment. After a few times, Fred figured out how to do it himself, and he started independently leading people to faith.

Since that time about thirty people have become

Christians largely under Fred's influence. He's now leading a small group in which he's teaching other believers to spread their faith like he does. Now some of them have recently had the thrill of leading their friends across the line of faith.

Fred is a direct, no-nonsense, hard-hitting businessman who is confrontational in his approach to evangelism. He enjoys the challenge of dealing with tough, nonreligious types whose lives are nearly scraping bottom and who don't know where else to look except up. Fred, needless to say, is a contagious Christian.

Julie, however, isn't anything like Fred. She's a shy, soft-spoken suburbanite, with two teenage daughters and a big, friendly dog. She and her husband, Bob, used to attend a comfortable, middle-of-the-road church where the gospel wasn't clearly taught.

Then one day through a series of events, Julie committed her life to Christ. She looked around for a biblically functioning church and decided to get involved at Willow Creek. Before long, she started rubbing shoulders with some outreach-minded members. And, like Fred, Julie attended the course in relational evangelism and got excited about impacting others with the gospel.

Since that time, she's helped her husband, parents, daughters, nephews, neighbours, and countless people she met at church become established in growing relationships with Christ. In one year alone, Julie personally led fourteen people in prayers of commitment to Him.

Due to Julie's introverted personality and unassuming approach, most people don't know what hit them. Our evangelism department refers to her as "God's secret weapon". It's interesting that part of what makes Julie so effective is that she in no way resembles the stereotypical evangelist. She's merely herself and, as a result, is successful in reaching others.

Contagious Christians can be found in a wide range of shapes, sizes, colours, ages, personalities, temperaments, and levels of experience. Just when you think you know what one looks like, a new variety comes along and breaks the mould.

Julie does have one thing in common with Fred: She, too, has become a contagious Christian. They're two special people. But they're also just ordinary Christians like you and me. They're merely sinners who've found the forgiveness of Christ and who have developed the values, character, and skills needed to impact the spiritual lives of others.

And just as these two differ from each other, contagious Christians can be found in a wide range of shapes, sizes, colours, ages, personalities, temperaments, and levels of experience. Just when you think you know what one looks like, a new variety comes along and breaks the mould.

This diversity becomes even more exciting when you realise that no two spiritual seekers look exactly alike, either. They come in many combinations of religious background, ethnicity, social standing, education, and level of openness to God, the church, and biblical teachings.

In His wisdom, God created all kinds of Christians and put them in circles of influence with all kinds of spiritual seekers. Through these circles, God's love and truth can be communicated in ways natural to both. But in order for that to happen, we need to learn the basics of spreading our faith and then to put what we've learned into action. After you do this for a while, and gain wisdom from mistakes along the way, you'll reach a point where you'll move from being awkward to graceful, from tentative to confident, from fearful to adventurous.

This is similar to learning any hobby, sport, or skill. There's always a degree of discomfort that goes with trying something new. Few skiers look impressive during their first run down the slope. Not many golfers blister the fairway on their first round. Or how about the first time you went roller skating? Remember your legs taking you in two directions at once?

After a few early bumps and bruises, some people quit, while others just try harder. Those who hang in there become more and more adept, and the activity becomes increasingly rewarding.

Becoming a contagious Christian is like that, too. The people who fall down in their efforts to build relationships and communicate the message of Christ, but who then get up, brush themselves off, and start over again can look forward to a day when they'll become confident and competent.

Fred and Julie are just two of many examples—and you could be another one.

Exponential effects

I've got a confession to make. I love seeing believers catch the vision of reaching lost people for Christ. It's great to see them get past their initial reluctance and develop levels of proficiency that, with the Holy Spirit's influence, will yield a bumper crop of new Christians. And I especially enjoy it when I hear that one of them has for the first time led someone to Christ, because I know that experience will expand their faith and ensure them even greater degrees of success.

But even more than this, I love seeing a few infectious believers spread the germ to others in their fellowship, who in turn pass it on to more people until an evangelistic epidemic erupts throughout their whole church.

Think about it: If *one* contagious Christian can be so effectively used by God, what happens when a whole *church* becomes contagious? When that occurs, we're talking explosive spiritual impact throughout the entire community. As important as our individual efforts are, ultimately God will reach the world through the combined strengths and activities of all of us in the church working together.

I don't need to tell you that most churches aren't like that. Thankfully, there are some shining exceptions, but far too many just go on week after week, trying to retain their numbers, meet their budgets, and maintain the status quo. They have no real vision for reaching lost people and showing them the way to God because they're too busy debating internal policies and dealing with all kinds of in-house strife.

I believe this is a travesty. That's not at all what Jesus had in mind when, in Matthew 16:18, He talked about building a church that the gates of hell would not overcome. His vision for the church was that it would be an active, dynamic, expanding force to be reckoned with (Acts 1:8). And central to its mission would be the rescuing, redeeming, and recruiting of people who are mired in sin.

With a mission of this magnitude, we all need to guard against complacency. Even if you're in a church that is in some measure striving for that goal, it's important not to focus on the number that have already been reached, but on the multitudes of hopeless people who will face God's judgment.

Yes, we should celebrate conversions when they occur, but we must never become satisfied and stop reaching out to others. Until the whole world has met Christ, we'll still have our work to do.

Characteristics of contagious churches

Don't you want to be involved in a church that wholeheartedly embraces this goal? Wouldn't you like to be part of an effort to make your church become more contagious? Well, to further your thinking on what that might look like, I'm going to list fifteen characteristics you'll find in evangelistically effective churches. Use them as a checklist to see whether they're true of the one you're a part of. My hope is that you and your fellow church members will not only appreciate your church's strengths, but also begin to discuss ways to deal with its weaknesses.

Evangelism is a basic value

Most people in churches can quote John 3:16. The fact that "God so loved the world" is not missing information among our ranks. The problem is that we can know it in our heads without letting it sink into our hearts. While it's theology to be believed, it must also become a value to be lived.

I've listed this characteristic first because it's where we most often fall down. Let me restate that: It's where *I* most often fall down. In spite of the fact that I've been teaching others for years that people matter to God, it's so easy for me to forget that fact when I get wrapped up in the middle of an intense work week. All of a sudden I'll catch myself treating someone as an object rather than as a person God loves and cares about.

The danger for leaders of would-be contagious churches is that they may overlook the need to continually reinforce this foundational value. Instead, they start new programmes, or experiment with the latest outreach trends, or, in frustration, they use guilt to try to push members into evangelism.

But the results of these approaches are usually shallow and temporary. Better to start with the basic beliefs of the congregation and, through teaching, illustrating, storytelling, discipling, and being an example, try to instill over time the heart of God toward irreligious people.

The fact that "God so loved the world" is not missing information among our ranks. The problem is that we can know it in our heads without letting it sink into our hearts. While it's theology to be believed, it must also become a value to be lived.

Lost people are prioritised

You can tell that a church values lost people by the way it sets priorities and makes decisions. This is especially true when the personal wishes of the members clash with the needs of spiritual seekers outside the church.

In the late 1960s, when the Jesus movement was starting to grow, traditional churches in southern California faced a dilemma. The problem was that long-haired, barefooted, hippy-types started coming into their worship services, and their dirty feet were soiling their sanctuaries' carpets.

Well, this caused a stir among the leaders of these churches. Some wanted to forbid these social outcasts from entering their buildings. But one pastor in particular, Chuck Smith, stood up and challenged that kind of thinking, declaring that these people should be loved and shown hospitality. Thankfully, his church accepted his wisdom on the matter. Calvary Chapel of Costa Mesa, California, is a ministry that has since touched the lives of thousands of spiritual seekers, and their approach to ministry has been replicated by other churches throughout the country.

Our own church faced a similar decision. The opportunity arose to host a debate between a well-known atheist and a highly respected Christian on the same day that a year-end celebration for our staff had already been scheduled. Although both events seemed important, we chose to defer to the one that had the potential to reach people for Christ. The debate ended up being one of the most exciting events in the history of the church, with almost eight thousand people in attendance and forty-seven people becoming believers right where they sat.

In hindsight it would be easy to say, "Well, of course people are worth far more than carpets, and evangelistic events more than parties. Why was there ever a question?" But it's not all that clear when priorities collide and church members dig in and defend their own pet concerns.

Lives will be changed after discussions in the car park, questions regarding the faith will be handled on the phone and in restaurants, ideas for new forms of outreach will be hatched in the hallways, and no one will be heard saying, "Oh, evangelism, that's so-and-so's job."

What takes precedence, for example, when the annual church picnic conflicts with the rare opportunity to put on an outreach-oriented event with a speaker who'll only be in town for that one day? Or what happens when the youth ministry needs money to stage an evangelistic concert for their friends, and you wanted to use those funds for painting the nursery or paving the car park—on top of the fact that you don't like the loud music those kids are playing anyway?

These are real conflicts of which you may already be painfully aware. Now do you see why I've started this list with the need to value evangelism and prioritise lost people? I'm not suggesting that these characteristics will provide cut-and-dried directives for every decision. But they are guiding principles that can keep in check our tendencies toward spiritualised self-centredness, and help us make decisions that will move our churches increasingly toward true contagiousness.

Outreach is a part of the overall strategy

Another important characteristic of these contagious churches is that outreach is an integrated element in their overall ministry strategy. In other words, evangelism training and events are not side-issues, relegated merely to one person, department, or night of the week. Rather, they're part-and-parcel of what the entire church is all about.

When this is the case, it'll be difficult to pin down exactly when or where "it" happens, because "it" will be happening all over the place. Lives will be changed after discussions in the car park, questions regarding the faith will be handled on the phone and in restaurants, ideas for new forms of outreach will be hatched in the hallways, and no one will be heard saying, "Oh, evangelism, that's so-and-so's job."

The seeking process is respected and facilitated

There's a danger for churches to turn the screws on any seeking visitor who walks in the door. "You might only get one chance," the thinking goes, "so you'd better seize it and lead them to Christ *now*."

What ends up happening is that the Christians intent on evangelising so intensively actually do get only one chance. But it's because they tried to seize the moment too quickly and lead the person to faith upon initial contact. The seeker simply gets scared away by their high-pressure tactics.

But there's something I've learned over my years in ministry. When you honour and validate the *process* people go through in coming to Christ, many of them will be willing to get started. Your approach tells them you really understand what they're going through as they take those difficult steps toward faith.

In my leadership, I've tried to allow for this seeking process in two primary ways. First, I encourage our members to build authentic relationships with people they hope to reach. That way they'll consistently be there as the friends go through the ups and downs of their spiritual journey.

Second, we've designed our weekend services to sensitively address the issues people face when they're investigating the Christian faith. We also let them know they won't be asked to sing, sign, say, or give anything while they're in their search phase. This allows them the opportunity they need to adequately honour Jesus' command to "count the cost" of following Him before they actually sign on the dotted line.

Seekers' questions are valued and addressed

One of the greatest fears that seekers face is being asked to commit to something they don't understand or agree with. Yet I hear from so many of them how a church leader embarrassed them for expressing honest doubts, or patronisingly told them that if they'd first accept Christian truth, then they'd find an inner assurance that it is, in fact, true. To a thoughtful seeker, these kinds of comments say, "These people don't care about truth. They're just trying to protect the party line. I'd better pack up and look elsewhere!"

The Bible tells us in 1 Peter 3:15 to "be prepared to give an answer to everyone who asks you to give the reason for the hope that you have." Furthermore, 1 Thessalonians 5:21 wants us to "test everything. Hold on to the good." We ought to be more concerned about truth than anyone, since we worship the God of truth and He commands us to study and know it for ourselves.

Churches that want to effectively reach honest truth-seekers will make concerted efforts to openly raise and address the questions people are asking. They'll exhibit confidence in the Bible and the beliefs they've staked their lives on, and that confidence will grow as they see how time and again the toughest challenges to the faith can be met with good answers.

The leaders model the reaching of lost people

"Do as I say and not as I do" is not a good way to build an outreach-oriented church. If people perceive that evangelism is just a platitude and not an actual practice of the leadership, exhortations to evangelise will go in one ear and out the other. The pastor, the elders, and any other staff members or visible leaders need to champion and model the value of spending time and energy in strategically relating to unchurched people.

This is especially true of the senior pastor. I know from experience how futile it is to challenge my listeners to do something that I'm not actively doing myself. It's impossible to speak with real conviction. The words fall powerless, sounding merely like nice ideas that somebody out there ought to try sometime.

Here, as elsewhere, the dictum holds true: "Speed of the leader, speed of the team." People in your church need to see you out in front, living an adventure-filled, action-packed lifestyle of rescuing the lost. They'll start saying to themselves, "Wow, if the pastor is willing to take some risks and invest himself in this, maybe it's time I started doing so, too."

The members are equipped to spread their faith

When modelling by leaders becomes commonplace, the people in the church will start looking for help in becoming more contagious themselves. In response to their hunger and enthusiasm, the church can offer practical forms of training that are designed to develop skills in effectively communicating the message of Christ.

This can be done in specialised classes and seminars, as well as in sermons from the pulpit and small group discussions. Members will attend without being coerced, because what they'll learn is relevant to a value that's already taken root in their hearts.

When that happens—when ordinary Christians

When ordinary Christians throughout the fabric of the church get trained and active in spreading their faith, you'd better watch out! A whole new era of activity and lifechange is going to explode. If you haven't experienced it before, you're about to feel the exhilaration of being part of a contagious church.

---

throughout the fabric of the church get trained and active in spreading their faith—*you'd better watch out!* A whole new era of activity and lifechange is going to explode. If you haven't experienced it before, you're about to feel the exhilaration of being part of a contagious church.

Relationships with unchurched people are maximised

In the training given at contagious churches, the importance of building authentic relationships with unchurched acquaintances is constantly underscored. This is where the battle will be won or lost. Without these friendships, we're inevitably back to the old hit-and-run tactics. These tactics might help a few, but they'll chase away many more.

In order to uphold the value of building these strategic relationships, contagious churches are careful not to overschedule the weekly calendar or subtly pressure their people to spend all their time at church-related functions. Rather, they honour the attempts of their members to spend quality time with people who need Christ.

These churches also allow for the kind of risk-taking Jesus engaged in when He went to the places irreligious people live. Realising there's danger in that, they encourage each other and hold one another accountable for maintaining a godly life.

Varied approaches to evangelism are celebrated

Contagious churches emphasise that effective evangelism looks just like their individual members. It can take forms that fit the personalities God has given them.

This is a radical departure from much of what has happened in recent decades. The tendency has been for a pastor to get charged up about doing outreach a certain way, and then to put subtle or even overt pressure on anyone else to imitate him. What ends up happening is that the few who are temperamentally similar to the leader flourish, but others try to force themselves to do things that don't fit them. Still others back away from the church completely, or they stay there and just feel guilty. They may say, "I wish I was a more spiritual person so I could do what they're doing."

In the process a lot of good people get hurt and, equally damaging, they don't get deployed to reach those who would have related to someone just like them. So high numbers of church members feel misunderstood and large segments of the population remain unreached.

Truly contagious churches avoid these problems by valuing many different approaches to the task of spreading the message. As members use their individual evangelistic styles and then combine strengths in a team, the church's outreach is bolstered tremendously.

For example, a woman called our church office recently out of concern for her husband who, she said, was in the process of becoming a Mormon. She didn't know how to help him see the problems in Mormonism in contrast to the truthfulness of biblical Christianity. So we supplemented her efforts with the intellectual approach of a couple of people in our apologetics ministry. They kept meeting with Rob until he came to the point of committing his life to Christ. Interestingly, he's now in that same ministry, utilising his own intellectual style to help others in the church reach those with similar issues.

Every position of service is viewed as part of the outreach of the church

In contagious churches, every position of service—regardless of the particular ministry it's a part of—is valued as an important contribution to the overall goal of reaching lost people.

The task itself might be to clean and maintain the building, operate the sound equipment, help people find a seat, teach and nurture the children, or balance the budget and pay the monthly bills. But each one adds to the evangelistic effectiveness of the church. As we all work together, we're able to do things to reach people that none of us could do alone. That makes every role vitally important.

The efforts of individual members are supplemented by larger outreach events

Even after the best of training and encouragement, the majority of church members will need help in bringing their friends all the way to the point of commitment. And while this can take many forms, one of the most strategic is to sponsor large outreach events to which they can bring their friends. It's amazing to see how even one well-designed service, concert, or programme can be used by God to replace mistaken notions about Him and to open seekers to hearing more.

Innovation, by the way, is not a new invention. Most dynamic movements in church history have been led by people who were willing to break the mould and try ministry a new way. Just look at the lives of such mavericks as Luther, Calvin, Wesley, Booth, and Moody.

Let me be clear that I'm not talking here about *worship* services, though they can be helpful to some seekers who are further along on their spiritual journey. I'm talking about events that are put together from top to bottom with nonbelieving friends in mind. These can take widely varied forms, from contemporary Christian concerts, to creative presentations that utilise drama, multimedia, and the arts, to mens' breakfasts, womens' luncheons, or leader's dinners in which a knowledgeable speaker gives a talk or testimony.

In the case of Willow Creek, each weekend we hold what we call our "seeker services", which present basic Christianity through a combination of music, drama, and a spoken message. We decided early in the formation of the church to hold these on Sunday mornings because that's when people in our neighbourhoods are most likely to visit a church. Then, as a next step, we offer worship services in the middle of the week, where believers come together to spend time exalting God, learning from His Word, and participating in communion.

Many other churches do similar seeker events on a different day of the week or with less frequency. It's important to maintain high quality, even if that means putting on fewer events. The point here is not to prescribe how many to have or what shape they should take, but to encourage churches to be strategic in efforts to win people to Christ. It's this combination of personal and corporate evangelistic efforts that can make a church highly contagious.

Innovation is valued and employed

As we saw earlier, Matthew didn't pick up his plan to have a banquet for his unbelieving buddies in the *First Century Manual of Approved Outreach Ideas*. Instead, he just looked at the need, assessed his abilities, got creative, and threw a party!

Churches that impact the culture around them make room for parties like Matthew's. They allow for new, innovative ideas for getting the message to those who need it. They take seriously Jesus' command in Mark 7 to avoid letting traditions get in the way of obeying God or ministering to people. Creativity is part of their thinking, and change is integral to their strategy. They're willing to take risks for the sake of those who are lost, but they learn from their mistakes and constantly readjust their course.

And when, in the process, they are misunderstood by fellow believers, as Jesus so often was, they listen and give prayerful consideration to their critics' words, but they also stay the course and finish the race, bringing as many new converts with them as possible.

Innovation, by the way, is not a new invention. Most dynamic movements in church history have been led by people who were willing to break the mould and try ministry a new way. Just look at the lives of such mavericks as Luther, Calvin, Wesley, Booth, and Moody. The challenge for us is not to get entrenched in the approaches *they* started, but to keep adjusting to constantly maximise our ministry impact.

The relevancy of the Bible is emphasised

Contagious churches realise that those outside the faith grossly underestimate the day-to-day benefits of knowing and honouring God. So they've learned to emphasise not only the central gospel message, but also the Bible's wisdom for everyday life, including guidance in the areas of marriage, child-raising, family and work relationships, conflict resolution, and issues related to ethics and morality. These churches know that as people find out that Christian teachings *work*, they'll stay around long enough to discover that Christian claims are also *true*.

These churches understand that they can't just teach doctrine and neglect the needs of practical living. But they also must avoid succumbing to the temptation to just pass around helpful advice without addressing the deeper issues of sin and salvation. This is not an either/or situation; it's both/and.

Contagious churches have learned that they must communicate to their culture without compromising with their culture. They know that if the message of the cross of Christ is ever diluted or hidden, then the battle has already been lost.

Jesus modelled this balance in Matthew 11:28–30. He started by saying, "Come to me, all you who are weary and burdened, and I will give you rest." To the tired and well-worn people He was addressing, this was a very appealing invitation. It was extremely relevant to them in their present situation. But He didn't stop there. He went on to tell them that if they'd follow and learn from Him, they would also find spiritual rest for their souls.

The gospel is never compromised

Contagious churches have learned that they must communicate *to* their culture without compromising *with* their culture. They know that if the message of the cross of Christ is ever diluted or hidden, then the battle has already been lost. What good is it to learn to speak the language of secular people if we lose our message in the process?

Some Christians have supposed that if a church wants to reach out to people, it must hold back from challenging them to make changes and yield their lives to God's control. In my experience, it's been almost exactly the opposite.

People are just plain tired of hearing lame, half-hearted appeals from religious leaders who lack the courage to shoot straight and tell them the truth. Many of them are looking for someone who'll give it to them without apology and dare them to stake their life on it. I've been surprised again and again that when I've pulled out the stops and confronted people to repent and trust Christ, many have thanked me for it and have done what I challenged them to do.

Now, this is an obvious manifestation of the Holy Spirit doing His work. But that's the point. He's ready to do His part and waiting for us to do ours. Contagious churches do just that, as they clearly and compellingly point people toward the salvation that's available only through Christ.

There's a tangible sense of the supernatural

There's a sense of wonder, similar to what's described in Acts 2, among the people involved in the kind of church I've been describing. And that, in itself, makes it become more contagious. God is clearly at work as miracle after miracle happens in the form of changed lives. Sceptics turn into seekers. Seekers find Christ. Christians develop confidence, and they become active and bold in communicating their faith. Intensity multiplies, while vision and the expectancy of further miracles expands. Churches affect other churches and even whole denominations, and soon an entire nation is moving toward God.

Through the Holy Spirit's power and the prayers and efforts of many contagious Christians, the goal of the formula—*maximum impact*—is fulfilled in amazing abundance.

To me, that's worth getting *excited* about. What could be more rewarding than being part of an enterprise like that? There are a lot of things I could live without, but this is not one of them. I'd sweep floors just to be around a contagious church.

But it all comes back to individuals: People like you and me, who know where to invest our lives. In one remaining chapter, I want to talk about the most strategic investment you'll ever make.

CHAPTER FIFTEEN

Investing Your Life in People

"We're here," the man said warmly to his wife. "Copacabana Beach, the top floor, a beautiful restaurant and a first-class hotel. It's been worth it, hasn't it, honey? Working and saving all these years were worth it for a night like tonight."

I couldn't help overhearing this couple at the table next to mine as I sat alone, thinking about all I'd seen over the previous few weeks. I was on the last leg of a month-long trip my father had sent me on throughout Central and South America to deliver money to missionaries he was supporting there. And since I was going that direction, he'd put together an itinerary with stops in several cities throughout South America, just so I could more fully experience that part of the world.

It was a very formative time in my life. I was nineteen years old. I'd recently become a Christian but didn't know yet what I was going to do for the rest of my life. I'd begun the journey with a tribe of Indians in the middle of the Central American jungle, where a church was flourishing. It was an exciting place. The Holy Spirit was active, and lives were being changed throughout the whole region.

From there I'd gone through several other cities, and ended up in Rio de Janeiro, Brazil, which at the time was the jet-set capital of the world. And now I was having dinner alone in an elegant restaurant, hearing this couple discuss how wonderful it was to finally be there.

I felt almost dizzy as I thought to myself, "Wait a minute. These people are about sixty years old, and they're saying they've waited a lifetime to experience *this*? I'm nineteen and I'm already sitting here! What am *I* going to do for the next thirty or forty years? If this is *It*, I'm in big trouble. It's nice, but it certainly isn't *It*."

I remember walking back to my room thinking, *What am I going to do with my life? What's important enough for me to invest my whole future in?*

As I reflected on the years I'd been working in my dad's company, many fond memories flashed through my mind. But I also sensed that it was not a career that would meet the yearning in my spirit to be part of something eternal and transforming.

By comparison, I thought back to that little church in the middle of the jungle, and the number of really sharp people who had given their lives to serve among those Indians. They'd built an amazing community of believers who were now leading their friends to Christ. I remembered sitting on the ground just days earlier during one of their worship services as they sang their hearts out in praise to God.

That night in Rio de Janeiro, I realised that what I'd seen happening in that tribe was more real, more lasting, and more important than just rolling up the score in the business world. And it was something I wanted to be part of.

As it turned out, that was a thought I was never able to shake, in spite of all the allurements and opportunities that would pull me in other directions.

The fishing business

It's an age-old struggle. I wasn't just wrestling with which profession to choose. I was grappling with where to invest my passion, dreams, and energy. I later realised that I was in good company when I read in the New Testament that some of Jesus' disciples wrestled with this issue, too.

Though fishermen by trade, Peter and Andrew had taken seriously Jesus' challenge in the fourth chapter of Matthew, where He had said to them, in effect, "I understand your preoccupation with catching fish. But hear me, fellas, and hear me well. If you'll trust me and follow me, if you'll try to understand who I am and what I'm up to in this world, then you'll also let me make you fishers of men. And believe me, this is infinitely more significant an endeavour than merely catching fish!"

It's important to understand that Jesus was not knocking the fishing business, any more than He would have knocked the construction business, from which He and Joseph had made a living. There's nothing wrong with those occupations, or the food business, the travel business, the insurance business, or the real estate business. They're all fine. But no earthly enterprise is as important as the business of bringing lost people to the cross of Christ. This should be central to the lives of all of His followers, regardless what they do for a career.

Those who choose to follow Christ will eventually come to the conclusion that there's nothing more important than reaching people. And when they do, their values will change forever. They'll be seized by the realisation that every other earthly activity pales in comparison with helping an individual man, woman, boy, or girl come into a saving, liberating, life-changing relationship with the God of the universe.

And once they understand that the most important

business in the world is the people business, watch out! They're going to live differently, pray differently, love differently, work differently, give differently, and serve differently, because they'll be preoccupied with people and their needs. They'll become consumed with how they can be more effective fishers of men.

Has this kind of thing happened to you yet? I was sitting in the sales office of my father's produce company in Michigan when I read some verses in the third chapter of 2 Peter that described the fiery fate of all the things I had been so concerned about getting. The thought just overwhelmed me; what a futile waste of effort to invest myself in obtaining so much temporal stuff.

Once they understand that the most important business in the world is the people business, watch out! They're going to live differently, pray differently, love differently, work differently, give differently, and serve differently, because they'll be preoccupied with people and their needs.

Then I remembered 1 Corinthians 9:25 where Paul said, "Everyone who competes in the games goes into strict training. They do it to get a crown that will not last; but we do it to get a crown that will last forever." Paul was saying, in effect, "They're all cranked up about the wrong race! I would rather that all of you believers trained and practiced and set your sights on winning the *real* race: the one that makes your life count for eternity by the way you serve God and the way you serve people."

Only a few of us will actually be asked to leave our nets and abandon our professions. Not many of us will be led by God to make ministry our career. The vast majority of Christians will be asked to function within their present occupations, but with a whole new mindset, one that reflects God's perspective on the eternal importance of people.

Like me, I'll bet you're thankful that the disciples chose to major in the people business rather than the fishing business. And I'll bet you're glad that in John 21, when Peter considered going back to catching fish, Jesus went to him and renewed His challenge to stay preoccupied with helping people. Three times He told Peter, "Stay with the people business."

That's what Peter did, and he was used by God to impact the entire world. In a much more modest way, that's also what I did, and I'm attempting to have an impact on my corner of the world. The only remaining question is, what will *you* do? Where will you invest your life?

Only a few of us will actually be asked to leave our nets and abandon our professions. The vast majority of Christians will be asked to function within their present occupations, but with a whole new mindset, one that reflects God's perspective on the eternal importance of people.

Let me implore you, for your own benefit and for the sake of your lost friends, if you love God with all your heart, soul, mind, and strength: *stick to the people business*. Say to the Holy Spirit each day, "Today, let me do more than merely catch fish. Help me do more than just sell a product. Inspire me to go beyond providing a service. Enable me to touch a human life. Work through me to reach a man or a woman for you. I want to be in the people business!" This is the mindset of a contagious Christian.

Jesus' final challenge

Before we conclude this last chapter, I'd like to repeat and apply the final challenge Jesus gave before finishing His earthly ministry and ascending into heaven. It's in Matthew 28:19–20: "Therefore go and make disciples of all nations, baptising them in the name of the Father and of the Son and of the Holy Spirit, and teaching them to obey everything I have commanded you. And surely I will be with you always, to the very end of the age."

Notice who Jesus was addressing. He was talking to His disciples, those who'd given up everything to follow Him and to become more like Him. Putting it in the terms of our formula, they had let His influence rub off on them to the point that they'd developed *highly potent* personalities. They'd received first-hand instruction and modelling from Jesus for living lives marked by authenticity, compassion, and sacrifice.

The second aspect of this challenge comes from the words, "go and make disciples of all nations." It's clear that Jesus wasn't expecting that to happen through diplomacy or political effort. Rather, it would come about as a result of their actually going and getting *in close proximity* to the people who they hoped to influence. In so doing, they'd have the opportunity to start relationships and naturally influence the people they'd come to know.

Next, Jesus emphasised that as they made disciples

they should teach them. While He was primarily referring to guiding new believers in spiritual growth and obedience to Christ, this guidance was certainly intended to be a continuation of the teaching that had been taking place all along. In other words, the teaching included *clear communication* of Christ's gospel message. The disciples would need to follow His example of initiating conversations on spiritual topics, spelling out the way to receive His salvation, and helping people overcome the barriers keeping them from belief.

Finally, Jesus promised He'd be with them—and us—"always, to the very end of the age." In addition to the guarantee of His presence and protection, this is an implicit assurance of what's explicitly stated elsewhere: that as we do our part in fulfilling this "great commission", He will do His part in making those efforts fruitful. In short, Jesus assured us that as we put His plan into action, we'll have *maximum impact* on our world around us. We'll see person after person crossing the line of faith, becoming contagious Christians, and joining increasingly contagious churches.

And that's good to know, isn't it? But my greatest fear for you is that you'll stop right there, merely having increased your knowledge about what it means to become a contagious Christian and what it takes to produce new ones. We both know that isn't enough.

Look one more time at those words of Jesus. All of the action He wants to initiate in the world begins with that small word, "go".

"Go," I can hear Him saying, "Spread the news that moral failures can be made right with God. Spread the news that repentant sinners can find grace and forgiveness. Spread the news that alienated men and women can be reconciled to God and each other. *Go*, and as you do, people will respond. And you'll know that you're doing your part in bringing about a worldwide renewal."

And I imagine that the eyes of Jesus' followers were like saucers. "Lord, worldwide renewal through the likes of *us*? Now, that's worth getting out of bed for every day. What a challenge! What a vision! You'd use us for *that*?"

It reminds me of the story of Steve Jobs, the co-founder of Apple Computers. He realised that the meteoric growth of his corporation necessitated the hiring of an experienced executive who could provide overall leadership. So he went after a top executive, John Sculley, who was with Pepsi-Cola.

After wining and dining him a bit, he started to get the sinking feeling that Sculley was going to turn down his offer. So he took him to the top of an apartment building overlooking Central Park in New York City, and made his final, last ditch effort to try to get him to join Apple.

Say to the Holy Spirit each day, "Today, let me do more than merely catch fish. Help me do more than just sell a product. Inspire me to go beyond providing a service. Enable me to touch a human life. Work through me to reach a man or a woman for you. I want to be in the people business!"

But even then it wasn't looking good. Finally, in total exasperation, Steve Jobs looked John Sculley in the eye and said to him, "Do you want to spend the rest of your life selling sugared water, or do you want a chance to change the world?"

In his book, Sculley writes that this challenge knocked

the wind out of him. And eventually it prompted him to leave PepsiCo and join Apple Computers.

Like John Sculley, all of us have a God-given yearning to change the world. But personal computers will never impact the world as much as leading someone into a personal relationship with Christ.

When a love-starved person is introduced to the grace of God for the first time, when a lonely person finally experiences the richness of companionship with Jesus Christ, when a guilty person finds forgiveness and a clean conscience, when a wandering person suddenly finds a purpose for his life, that's *impact*. And a powerful chain reaction is set into motion.

That person impacts people in his world. A husband affects his wife. Parents influence their children. Friends tell friends. Coworkers clue in colleagues. Little networks of Christians are formed. Churches are established and strengthened. New ministries are launched. And pretty soon, there's new life breaking out all over the place. The poor start getting cared for, the hungry are fed, the sick are visited, the lonely are loved, the wounded are helped toward wholeness. Before you know it, that corner of the world has changed just a little bit.

But a chain reaction must be started by someone who's willing to *go*. Someone who's willing to step out of their comfort zone to create some action. Someone who's willing to say a word for the risen Saviour without shrinking back. In a very real way, worldwide change hinges on that one verb in Jesus' commandment: *go*.

Isn't today a good day to mark as the day you decided that there's more to life than just selling sugar water? Wouldn't this be an ideal day to say to God, "With your help, I'll *go*, and I'll start some chain reactions in my world. By your power, we'll change some lives"? Getting started isn't easy, but it's worth it, and you'll never regret throwing yourself into building His kingdom.

Wisdom from the aged

A recent survey asked people who were ninety-five years or older what they'd do differently if they could live their lives over. Their responses were very pertinent to our topic. Here are the top three changes these people listed.

They'd reflect more

They would spend more time getting away from the daily grind in order to thoughtfully examine the direction and meaning of their lives. In so doing, they'd make certain the energy they were expending was going toward worthwhile causes.

Can I challenge you to do the same, especially as it relates to becoming a more contagious Christian? Take time to look back through this book and to ask yourself how you're doing in each part of the formula. Are you developing a highly potent character that will attract people to Christ? Where might you need to concentrate some extra effort?

They'd risk more

Given another chance, these elderly people made it clear they'd be more courageous about stepping out of their comfort zones. They'd take risks in order to raise their accomplishment level and make life more interesting.

How about you? This life is your only chance to do just that. And where could you more strategically take risks than in the area of spreading the faith, which carries with it so many rewards for everyone involved?

Your Christian life will never be the exciting adventure I've been describing unless you're willing to get out on the limb of faith and humbly watch God fulfil His promises to guide, protect, and use you in His kingdom-expansion efforts.

This is a lesson that Greg, a relatively new Christian at our church, learned in trying to communicate his faith to a sceptical family member. Greg called Mark and told him, "I've concluded that the only way to really learn this whole personal evangelism thing is to just go out and get bloodied. The best way to find the holes in your armour is to get out there and use it!"

There's a lot of truth in what he's saying. You've read this book, you've reflected on a course of action and now, ready or not, you've got to get on the front lines of the battle and fight for the sake of some loved ones. You might get injured, but you'll see personal growth and increasing evangelistic effectiveness in the process. And when you're ninety-five years old, you'll be glad you took some risks and didn't hold back!

They'd do more things that will outlive them

Do I even need to comment on this one? Sure, there are some things that we can invest our lives in that will last incrementally longer than our own sixty to eighty years. But consider the spiritual returns on *eternal* investments. A chain reaction you start today could continue well into the next century and even to Christ's return. Think of the impact in heaven! What could be more exciting or rewarding than that?

It was a dark era in my life. I'd blown out my Achilles tendon while playing football with a bunch of raucous unchurched guys I was building relationships with. I'd had surgery to rejoin the severed tendon, but it wasn't healing properly. In fact, it was causing me so much pain that they had to go in and reopen the wound to make sure everything was all right.

After lying in the hospital for almost a week, I was

finally released. And although Lynne and I got away to try to rest and recuperate, I was hurting on the outside and in a mild state of depression on the inside.

Then the telephone rang. It was a long-distance call from my sailing friend, Tom, who was phoning from the Virgin Islands between sailing trips.

"Well, I did it!" he said enthusiastically.

My first thought was that he'd wrecked my friend's boat that I'd lined up for him to use. "What do you mean, 'you did it'?" I asked.

"I gave my life to Christ," he explained. "I prayed with John, one of the guys from your church who came with me on last week's trip."

I almost couldn't believe it. After nearly three years of trying to teach, challenge, motivate, and inspire this unlikely candidate for conversion, he'd finally stepped across the line of faith. What an incredible encouragement at such a low time in my life!

Your Christian life will never be the exciting adventure I've been describing unless you're willing to get out on the limb of faith and humbly watch God fulfil His promises to guide, protect, and use you in His kingdom-expansion efforts.

Since then, it's been a thrill to watch Tom's attitudes and values change. He's still as competitive and full of life as ever, but he's not as out-of-control as he was in the past. He now has an inner drive and purpose he never exhibited before.

Don't get me wrong: he still has some rough edges. But

he's honest, and he's sincerely trying to find out what it means to live a life that's pleasing to God.

Not too long ago, for example, he was at a crew party that I heard about later. Evidently he had too much to drink and got a little carried away. But soon afterwards, he wrote a letter of apology to every member of the crew. He told them that this sort of behaviour was inconsistent with the commitment to Christ he'd recently made, and he asked them for their forgiveness. I can only imagine the impact that must have had on them!

One of Tom's friends who saw the changes in him thought, at first, that he was just going through a phase. Then he got worried that Tom would get carried away and become a religious fanatic. But over time he actually begin to appreciate some aspects of the new Tom, like stability, direction, and fewer destructive patterns.

Tom's friend grew curious. The two of them started getting together and having deep conversations about these issues. Tom answered all of his friend's questions that he could, and then encouraged him to talk to me and others who could assist in articulating the truths of the Christian faith. Tom even drove his friend all the way from Michigan to the suburbs of Chicago in order to take him to a service at our church! It was a strategic step. They stayed in our home, and we had long talks into the night.

Since then, Tom, his friend, and I have had other serious conversations together about the gospel and its implications for our lives. Tom's friend is opening up, but he's not ready to step across the line of faith.

Not yet. But Tom and I keep praying.

Can you see why I told you at the very beginning that there's nothing as exciting in life as befriending, loving, and leading wayward people toward faith in Christ? There's no adventure like it, and no other activity that comes even close to offering the same level of rewards.

I'm thrilled to see that Tom—infectious, gregarious, on-the-edge Tom—is becoming a contagious Christian. And I'm looking forward to the day when his friend will join the family and, in turn, partner with us in the effort to spread God's love and truth to more and more people.

How about you? Are you on that team? Are you willing to take risks and put into action what you've learned about communicating the message of Christ?

Let me close with part of a letter I recently received from Tom. As you read it, think about the people you'd like to reach for Christ. Imagine this letter someday coming to you from one of them, and let it motivate you to do everything necessary to become a genuinely contagious Christian.

Dear Bill:

I want to take the time to thank you for all your help, spiritually and as a friend. I really enjoy our times of fellowship and the challenges you've given me. I pray that our friendship will keep growing and that you'll continue to challenge me.

It has been almost a year since I gave my life to Christ. I would never have dreamed that my life would change like this. God does listen to me and care for me, and I feel His presence. When I don't follow His lead I really know it. Each day is a new adventure, and I look forward to every one.

Thanks again,
Tom